Where Are the Davids?

Dare to Become the Leader That God Created You to Be

DAVID AYER

WESTBOW
P R E S S®
A DIVISION OF THOMAS NELSON
& ZONDERVAN

Scripture quotations are from the ESV® Bible (The Holy Bible, English Standard Version®), copyright © 2001 by Crossway, a publishing ministry of Good News Publishers. Used by permission. All rights reserved.

THE HOLY BIBLE, NEW INTERNATIONAL VERSION®, NIV® Copyright © 1973, 1978, 1984, 2011 by Biblica, Inc.® Used by permission. All rights reserved worldwide.

Scripture taken from the King James Version of the Bible.

Scripture taken from the NEW AMERICAN STANDARD BIBLE®, Copyright © 1960, 1962, 1963, 1968, 1971, 1972, 1973, 1975, 1977, 1995 by The Lockman Foundation. Used by permission.

WestBow Press books may be ordered through booksellers or by contacting:

WestBow Press
A Division of Thomas Nelson & Zondervan
1663 Liberty Drive
Bloomington, IN 47403
www.westbowpress.com
1 (866) 928-1240

Because of the dynamic nature of the Internet, any web addresses or links contained in this book may have changed since publication and may no longer be valid. The views expressed in this work are solely those of the author and do not necessarily reflect the views of the publisher, and the publisher hereby disclaims any responsibility for them.

Any people depicted in stock imagery provided by Getty Images are models, and such images are being used for illustrative purposes only. Certain stock imagery © Getty Images.

ISBN: 978-1-9736-4759-1 (sc)
ISBN: 978-1-9736-4760-7 (hc)
ISBN: 978-1-9736-4758-4 (e)

Library of Congress Control Number: 2018914571

Print information available on the last page.

WestBow Press rev. date: 1/17/2019

DEDICATION

To the three amazing women who have taken this journey with me: My wife, Denise and my daughters, Gavrielle and Moriyah.

My precious Denise, I could not have made it without you. Thank you for making me better than I ever could have been without you. Thank you for never quitting on us or the calling that we share. I love you.

David

Gavi & Mari, I know it's been hard. I know that too often you didn't understand why. My prayer is that your faith has grown and that you too will each become A David. Serve Jesus. It is the best life. I love each of you more than you could ever know.

Daddy/Papa/Fritas

I'd like to say a very special thank you to Dad and Kathy. Without you, this project would have been impossible. Thank you for believing in it. Here it is.

CONTENTS

PREFACE

No book was ever written by accident, so why do you hold this book in your hands? Because I wanted to give you something that I never had. I want to give you a road map—a road map to your destiny.

God made you. He crafted you with purpose. Inside you, inside your DNA, are not just the codings of hair color, height, athletic ability, intelligence, or any other such things. Those are just the things we can see and measure. No, in your very makeup are the seeds of greatness that God intended for you to cultivate and grow to bring His light into this dark world, but look around you. Do you see much light? Do you see much greatness? Do you look at many people and say, "Wow! They were made for that"? Unless you live on a different planet than I do, the answer is no. Most people never become more than casual livers of life, observers of the ordinary, and experiencers of the usual, but is that what God intended?

This book is a recipe for rebellion against the ordinary life. Is it a road map to destiny? Yes, but that is really just a rose-colored metaphor. This book is really a compass and a machete because that's all you need to move forward. You see, in this book I'm giving you True North and a tool to cut away the obstacles that you will face on your journey. What's awesome is that inside you (are you ready for this?), God has already set your destination. You feel that, don't you? Like something deep inside you wants to pull you into something truly *great*, but you just don't know what it is? It's there, and you are going to discover it. More than that, with your trusty compass and your sharp machete, you are going to get there. In this book, each chapter is like a refueling station on your journey, providing you with needed supplies and the coordinates of your next stop. It's a hard path. Your arms will get tired from clearing the way before you, and at times you will feel completely lost. You can quit at any time, but you know in your heart of hearts that *that* decision only guarantees that you will never see your destiny fulfilled, so keep going. If you do, you too will become ... A David.

Where Are The Davids?

INTRODUCTION

What is a David? The better question is, Who was David? If you live in the US or UK, there's a good chance that you don't really know. You might have heard of David right before a mismatched athletic contest, where the commentator said something like, "This is a real David-and-Goliath matchup." This usually happens right before the "David" gets completely mauled, mutilated, and destroyed by the "Goliath." Why? Because David isn't supposed to win. If you've ever read the story of David in your Bible, however, you know something interesting … he does.

When we find David, he's young, about sixteen years old. This handsome and athletic but basically normal teen is out on a sun-scorched field, facing the warrior-giant named Goliath, who carries a shield the size of Texas and a spear you could drive into the ground and stick a regulation basketball hoop on. This is the original David vs. Goliath matchup. So how does David come out for battle? Did he come out to face this monster of a man in the most high-tech armored chariot that Israel could produce? Did he roll out wearing the most sophisticated new body armor sent down from heaven on special delivery just for him? No, he went out carrying nothing but a shepherd's staff, a sling, and a bag of five stones, but is that all that he had? No. He had a secret weapon, one that no one could see or could even guess that he possessed. He had his God.

David is one of the great heroes of the Bible for one reason— because he stepped out into battle against impossible odds for the honor and glory of God—and he won.

Where Are The Davids?

Today, Western Christianity is in a battle as never before. In the nation that pioneered the world missions movement, Great Britain, it is estimated that almost 40 percent of people don't believe in God. The United States, another cornerstone of Christianity for the last three hundred years, is not too far behind, with 20 percent of the Americans saying they have "no religious affiliation." On the surface, that looks good. That means that 80 percent of Americans see themselves as holding at least some kind of faith in God. That's good, right? Yeah, but only 20 percent of Americans go to worship services of any kind outside of the holidays. That means *only* 25 percent (20/80 from above) of those who actually claim a faith of *any kind* (we aren't talking just Christians here) actually express that faith in worship on a given Sunday. Not only that, but Christian marriages are ending almost as fast as non-Christian marriages; priests and pastors have destroyed lives through sexual misconduct; and an alarming percentage of our Christian men and women are addicted to porn, and these are just the obvious problems. All this is going on while militant atheists are trying to "evangelize" our schools and societal systems to the "evils" of religion. It is in *this* moment in history that you find yourself right now.

As you read this book, you are the generation on the battlefield that is staring down at the enormous giant that has declared war against the church and her Christ. It is in this moment that I hear a call on the wind … the voice rumbling in the distance. What is it? Where is it coming from? You hear it too, don't you? You've strained to hear its message. It is a voice coming from deep within the heart of God, a voice that asks, "Where are the Davids?"

You Are A David

There are a ton of things in this world trying to tell you who or what you are. It can be that kid who sits behind you in school, mocking as he grades your paper, or the bully on the playground, at the gym, or in your home who tells you, "You're nothing." The truth is, it's anyone who tries to limit you to his or her definition of you. These are your giants. You could believe them—that's your choice. That was the choice of David's brothers and the others in the army of Israel when they faced Goliath. The giant said he was going to tear them apart and feed what was left of their bodies to the desert wildlife, and they believed him! You see, that's the power of the words of the giant. It's not that he said those words. It's not even that he could do what he said. It's that *they believed* he would do it. But David didn't believe the giant's words. Instead, he believed the words that God had spoken about him when He sent the old prophet Samuel to David's house and named him the next king of Israel!

God sees you. He knows your destiny because He knows exactly what He put inside you on the day you were conceived. He knows that inside, you are a king.

Where Are The Davids?

David was not just a king. Of all the kings that would ever be, he was *the* king, but even that was not all he was. He was also a priest and a prophet. In fact, he was the first king/priest/prophet in history. You may wonder who the others are. Jesus is the next and obviously supreme King/Priest/Prophet (read 1 Timothy 6:13b–16; Matthew 21:10–11; Hebrews 4:14–15). It isn't a coincidence that Jesus was called the "Son of David" (Matthew 9:27; Luke 18:38–39). That statement comes to us not only because He comes from David's family line (and so is the natural heir to David's earthly throne but that's the subject of another book) but because He is the fullest expression of David's position before God. The scriptures call Him the King of kings, our Great High Priest, and the Prophet from Nazareth! He became our Savior when He, the Son of David, faced the giants of sin, death, and Satan on the cross and rose victorious over them that Easter morning.

While that is still in your head, I want you to remember *why* Jesus came. In the fourth century Athanasios of Alexandria wrote, "God became man so that we might become children of God." Put another way, Jesus, the Son of God, became what we were so that we could become what He is: God's sons and daughters.

Jesus is the supreme King/Priest/Prophet, but He's not the last one; *we are.* As children of God through our faith in Jesus Christ, we are all kings/prophets/priests called by God to save this world from its giants (Revelation 1:6; Romans 5:17; 1 Peter 2:9; Acts 2:14–18). That is why the Bible calls us "joint heirs" or "co-heirs with Christ."

> The Spirit himself testifies with our spirit that we are God's children. Now if we are children, then we are heirs—heirs of God and co-heirs with Christ, if indeed we share in his sufferings in order that we may also share in his glory. (Romans 8:16–17)

Being an heir is about receiving an inheritance. In the end, being the heir to a king is about inheriting and stepping into that king's authority to help to extend his rule. It is this authority that moved David with each step forward as he walked onto the battlefield to face the giant. He wasn't going out there alone with just a sling and a few stones. No, he was going out there with the ultimate "David." The eternal champion, the King of Kings and the Lord of Lords was by his side. Yes, he faced the giant, but not as a mere shepherd boy. David walked onto the battlefield as the future king of Israel, with all of heaven backing him up.

What giant are you facing? Are you hiding because you're intimidated by its size and paralyzed by its ferocity? Face your giants. Stand strong. Know who is with you. Step out onto the battlefield. This book will help to show you how.

Where Are The Davids?

SECTION 1

HEART

The Prerequisite to Becoming A David

What makes A David? What made God call him out of the sheep pasture that cold, dark night? His brothers had all stood before the prophet, with his ram's horn filled with oil, ready to christen the next king, yet they all had been passed over. It made no sense to Samuel. Eliab, David's oldest brother, was so impressive that Samuel said, "Surely this is the next king," but he wasn't. Neither was the next one or the one after that. After the last of the seven brothers was passed over, the prophet raised his head and asked, "Is there another?"

Why did God pass over these impressive men? God said to Samuel, "The Lord does not look at the things people look at. People look at the outward appearance, but the Lord looks at the heart" (1 Samuel 16:7b). So it's not your abilities, looks, brains, or anything else that makes you A David. It's your heart. And it was David's heart that made God call him out of obscurity to receive the anointing to become Israel's king.

The heart is the prerequisite. It is the foundation that all other learning, training, and purifying will be added to, to create the life God intended you to live. These pages will give you the elements of the heart of A David. Don't blow by this section, thinking you want to get to the "good stuff." To God, *this is the good stuff*. God can always give you anything you ever need to fulfill His purpose for your life, but He can't fix a heart that's not His. Because of that, this is the most important section of this book. Honestly, if you come to own the heart of A David revealed in this section, God will bring you the rest. Here's my advice: as you read each of the chapters in this section, be determined to bring your heart into *that place* with God. If you are there, great … but most of you aren't, and even those of you who might be will need more. Pray yourself into these places of the soul. Study God's Word and find His heart so that you make it your own. If you don't, you can go no further. Remember, the heart is the foundation. It is the prerequisite for everything else that God wants to bring into your life. Without the heart of A David, there is no David.

Where are the Davids?

CHAPTER 1

Heart of Worship

Enthroning the King

Yet you are holy, enthroned on the praises of Israel.

—Psalm 22:3

Question: What is worship?

Answer: Worship is an opportunity to enthrone God, the King.

For many of us, worship is this thing we do on Sundays before we hear the preaching. It's like the fifteen minutes of previews at the theater that might capture our interest (or not). I have a crazy schedule, so if I get to catch a movie, I'm usually running later than the showtime, but I'll say, "It's all right. We'll only miss the previews." You see, previews are always viewed as optional. Many in the church today look at worship in the same way. Worship is nice. We may even enjoy engaging in the singing, but most consider it the preliminaries before we get to the "main event," IE the preaching. Sadly, that's not how God sees it. Worship is the real reason anyone ever comes to church—or comes to God, for that matter. The fact is, worship is all we really have to give to the God who has everything.

Enthroning God

What's the significance of "enthroning God"? Why should it matter whether or not God is enthroned in our worship? The simple answer is this: God is the King. When we create a throne for Him in our midst, we invite Him to reign here on the earth among, through, and with His people—and in case you forgot, that's us.

Worship for God's people is crucial not just on Sunday morning but every day and in every way. Our worship is really an invitation to God to join us and reign among us. We need to know this. Some victories can be won only through worship.

Life Lesson: Some victories can be won only through worship.

In 2 Chronicles, there is a story of one such battle.

> "Hear me, Judah and inhabitants of Jerusalem! Believe in the LORD your God, and you will be established; believe his prophets, and you will succeed." And when he had taken counsel with the people, he appointed those who were to sing to

the LORD and praise him in holy attire, as they went before the army, and say, "Give thanks to the LORD, for his steadfast love endures forever."

And when they began to sing and praise, the LORD set an ambush against the men of Ammon, Moab, and Mount Seir, who had come against Judah, so that they were routed. (2 Chronicles 20:20b–22)

Did you catch that? God won the victory without a sword drawn or a spear thrown. God routed the enemy all by Himself as His people worshipped Him. I have been in worship services where the Spirit of God came into the room so powerfully that people were healed during the worship. Why? Because God was there, extending His reign into the room. You see, where God's kingdom is, there is no sickness or disease. There is only His victory.

David's Heart

David's heart was a heart of worship. David was, in fact, a songwriter. You have probably heard of the book of Psalms. Psalms is a kind of worship book of the nation of Israel. David wrote more than half of the psalms. Worship is the foundation of David's ministry. We don't know when David began writing Psalms, but it's safe to assume that it was well before he was anointed to be the next king of Israel. Before David was anointed to be king (1 Samuel 16:13), he was already an accomplished musician, to the point that he was asked to play for King Saul, the king of Israel at the time (1 Samuel 16:16–19).

So Saul said to his servants, "Provide for me a man who can play well and bring him to me." One of the young men answered, "Behold, I have seen a son of Jesse the Bethlehemite, who is skillful in playing, a man of valor, a man of war, prudent in speech, and a man of good presence, and the LORD is with him." Therefore Saul sent messengers to Jesse and said, "Send me David your son, who is with the sheep" (1 Samuel 16:17–19).

Did you catch that? Because this is important. David was a shepherd. His place was in a field, watching stinky sheep, yet this shepherd boy was given an engraved invitation to come to the palace. This invitation was not to be the janitor or a cook. No, David was invited to the throne room itself to be the court musician. It wasn't David's anointing to be the next king of Israel that got him there (I mean, that would make sense, right?). But no, it was David's *worship* that got him invited into the palace.

Life Lesson: Your worship will get you invited to places that in the "real world" that you should never have been able to access.

Worship is powerful because it connects you with God personally. Worship is inter-dimensional. It literally allows you to cross from the physical world of time and space into eternity where only God lives. It is here that we meet with our Father and connect with Him past all limits. As we reach up to Him, He comes down to us and the relationship grows. Ultimately, worship is about our making time to develop the most important relationship in our lives: our relationship with God.

Developing a Worship Point of View

Deep worship changes everything because it changes what we see. Worship is about looking into the greatness of God and then telling Him what we are seeing. Often, that is about how awesome He is, and, just like any father, He likes to know that His children think He *totally rocks*—but it's a lot more than that. When we look into His greatness, it changes us. We begin to see as we haven't seen before. Our faith begins to grow. We feel emboldened to stretch, to reach, to achieve, and even to risk greatly because we have confidence in the God who is our Father.

Most of us know the story of David and Goliath. Goliath was a beast! He was somewhere around twelve feet tall. Not only was he a giant, but he was also a warrior. When David went to King Saul to ask permission to face the giant on the battlefield, the king said that Goliath had been a successful warrior from his earliest years, but this didn't sway David. Worship had changed his perspective. It's not that David didn't see the mountain of a man who stood tauntingly on the battlefield. It's that he saw the God who was with him. Goliath was huge, but he was nothing compared to the one who was going onto the battlefield with David.

Life Lesson: A heart that has been stretched through worship can believe in God for the impossible.

Where's Your Heart?

Worship is more than "song service" or a "worship set." Worship is a life lived for God. David lived for God, and worshipping Him was the beat of his heart—and *that* is the key because to God, the passion of our hearts is everything. The Bible reveals that the heart is the center of all a person's desires, whether that is evil (Matthew 15:17–20) or good (Luke 6:45). Because of this, the man that God chose to rule over His people had to have a heart like His. Look at what God says about why He chose David:

> Samuel said to Saul, "You have acted foolishly; you have not kept the commandment of the LORD your God, which He commanded you, for now the LORD would have established your kingdom over Israel forever." But now your kingdom shall not endure. *The LORD has sought out for Himself a man after His own heart*, and the LORD has appointed him as ruler over His people, because you have not kept what the LORD commanded you." (1 Samuel 13:13–14, my emphasis)

> When they arrived, Samuel saw Eliab and thought, "Surely the Lord's anointed stands here before the Lord." But the Lord said to Samuel, "Do not consider his appearance or his height, for I have rejected him. The Lord does not look at the things people look at. People look at the outward

appearance, but *the Lord looks at the heart.*" (1 Samuel 16:6–7, my emphasis)

After removing Saul, he made David their king. God testified concerning him: "I have found David son of Jesse, a man *after my own heart*; he will do everything I want him to do." (Acts 13:22, my emphasis)

Life Lesson: God must rule the man who is to rule His people.

This is pretty simple, really. Before God can trust a man to rule for Him, He must know that He rules in him. David enthroned God through a life of worship long before David was enthroned to rule over Israel.

Principle 1: A David is a worshipper.

Worship is not only about what you do on Sunday morning. Worship is how you live every day, in every way.

Where are the Davids?

CHAPTER 2

Heart of a Shepherd

Then all the tribes of Israel came to David at Hebron and said, "Behold, we are your bone and flesh. In times past, when Saul was king over us, it was you who led out and brought in Israel. And the LORD said to you, 'You shall be shepherd of my people Israel, and you shall be prince over Israel.'" So all the elders of Israel came to the king at Hebron, and King David made a covenant with them at Hebron before the LORD, and they anointed David king over Israel.

—2 Samuel 5:1–3

Question: Why David?

Answer: He had a shepherd's heart.

What was the "X factor" that caused David to be chosen king? Remember, he was a boy or at most a young adult. He was not even twenty years old. He'd never been in a battle. This dude was barely shaving, so how could God pick him to be king over all the warriors in Israel? Have you ever asked that question? I did—until I realized that the answer is more obvious than most of us realize: David was a shepherd.

According to the *Merriam-Webster Dictionary*, a shepherd is a person who tends sheep. If this is not on your list of educational expectations for the position of king, then you may want to take a pointer from the God of heaven because it seems like this is at the top of His list. To really understand this, we need to look at David's predecessor a little more closely.

Saul was a child of privilege. He came from a wealthy farming family, and it seems that he might have herded the family's donkeys as a young man. Donkeys are stubborn, willful, and lazy. Translation: They want to do what they want. Though true, their value to their owners is that once you get them going, they work hard. The key is to get them working. That combination means one thing: Donkeys need to be driven! If you look at the reign of Saul, that is exactly how he ruled. He either drove the people or let them do what they wanted. He treated them like the donkeys of his youth. To Saul, God's people were either a tool to get what he wanted or a nuisance to be left to their own devices until they become useful to him again.

David was a shepherd. Shepherds care for sheep. Sheep, by the way, are dumb, gentle animals, cultivated for their wool, milk, and meat. They have no natural defenses, and so they need to be led, cared for, and protected. Translation: They need a good shepherd. That is how David ruled. God didn't need a bipolar, insecure, power-monger to drive His people. He wanted a shepherd. He wanted a man like Him.

God is a shepherd. Many times in the scriptures, the Lord is referred to in this way:

> He blessed Joseph, and said, "The God before whom my fathers Abraham and Isaac walked, The God who has been my shepherd all my life to this day, The angel who has redeemed me from all evil, Bless the lads; And may my name live on in them." (Genesis 48:15–16)

> But his bow remained steady, his strong arms stayed limber, because of the hand of the Mighty One of Jacob, because of the Shepherd, the Rock of Israel. (Genesis 49:24)

> The LORD is my shepherd, I lack nothing. (Psalm 23:1)

> He tends his flock like a shepherd: He gathers the lambs in his arms and carries them close to his heart; he gently leads those that have young. (Isaiah 40:11)

> Hear the word of the LORD, O nations, and declare it in the coastlands far away; say, 'He who

scattered Israel will gather him, and will keep him
as a shepherd keeps his flock.' (Jeremiah 31:10–17)

The LORD their God will save his people on that
day as a shepherd saves his flock. They will sparkle
in his land like jewels in a crown. (Zechariah
9:16)

God Is Israel's Shepherd

It was the heart of a shepherd that qualified David to rule. Above
all the able-bodied, trained soldiers of Israel, God chose David. You
see, God's call to reign is not for the talented or the trained. Too
often we forget that it is God Himself who brings the victory to His
people. Lack of talents or abilities is something God makes up for
every day by this thing called grace. Talent is never the issue. The
one thing that God can't supply is the one thing that matters most
in His eyes: a heart like His. The Lord said to Saul, "But now your
kingdom will not endure; the LORD has sought out a man after his
own heart and appointed him ruler of his people, because you have
not kept the LORD's command" (1 Samuel 13:14).

In the New Testament we find out that this is exactly what
qualified David to be king. He was a man after God's own heart.

After removing Saul, he made David their king.
God testified concerning him: 'I have found
David son of Jesse, a man after my own heart; he
will do everything I want him to do.' (Acts 13:22)

This is also what qualifies us. Later, we find that Jesus is the Good Shepherd (John 10:11, 14), and so God calls us "shepherds" under the leadership of Jesus Christ, the Chief Shepherd (1 Peter 5:1–5). As you move through this book in your quest to become a David, you need to remember one thing: If God is ever to truly establish you in the calling/throne which He created you for, you will need to learn to love sheep. God isn't looking for someone to rule over His people. He got that in Saul. God wants a shepherd to lead and protect His people.

Listen to these words spoken to David on the day he was anointed king over Israel:

> In times past, when Saul was king over us, it was you who led out and brought in Israel. And the LORD said to you, '*You shall be shepherd of my people Israel*, and you shall be prince over Israel.' (2 Samuel 5:2 emphasis mine)

Principle 2: A David is a shepherd.

He develops a heart of love and care for those he leads. This love is not a sign of weakness. In fact, that love is why you were chosen, because that kind of heart reflects the heart of God toward His people.

Where are the Davids?

CHAPTER 3

Heart for God

He (God) raised up David to be their king, of whom he testified and said, 'I have found in David the son of Jesse a man after my heart, who will do all my will.'

—Acts 13:22b

David loved God. His heart was not just for his people but for the God of his people. This love is heard in the artful expression of the psalms David wrote; it's recognized in his wild abandon in worship, but mostly it is seen in the life he lived.

Life Lesson: Love for God will produce a life lived for God.

David was anointed. The old prophet poured oil over David's head and declared him to be the next king of Israel, but after the ceremony was finished, he had to go back to the field and watch over his father's sheep.

Life Lesson: One of the hardest places in life
is to be called to the throne in the palace but
instead be stuck in the field watching sheep.

A hard lesson is that a calling from God doesn't cancel your other responsibilities. So often when we feel called, we are ready to "hit the road" and do that thing that we were created to do, but that's not how this works. God doesn't usually want you to sell everything and live in the back seat of your car. Most times He just wants you to keep doing what you are doing. After all, what you are doing put you in position to receive this calling in the first place so just keep "watching Daddy's sheep" and allow God to raise you up. He knows you can't fulfill your calling sitting in a field. If you keep your heart focused on the Lord, your time will come.

Early one morning, while still watching the sheep, his father called him over. "David, I need you to bring these supplies to your brothers." Eliab and his other older brothers had left days earlier to fight against the Philistines as part of Saul's army. David wasn't sent to the battle. The Law said that he had to be at least twenty years old to fight in Israel's army. David may have been too young to serve in the army, but he wasn't too young to serve his father and his brothers. It was his willingness to serve that sent him to the battlefront that day, not with a sword but with corn, bread, and cheese for his brothers and their commanders. Most of us aren't crowned from birth. We earn a place of honor by serving. Are you called to be king? Great! Now prove it by serving.

Life Lesson: Serve your brothers, your nation, and your world. Serving—not selfishness or self-exaltation—brings us to our destinies.

When David got there with the supplies, he heard the challenge of a man twice his size. "Send out a man for me to fight!" Yet nobody moved. The giant hissed a challenge: "Come out and fight me. It's winner takes all. If you defeat me, we will be your slaves, but if I win, you will serve us." Still nobody moved. Then this man did the unthinkable and defied God himself. David had enough. "Who is this man that he should defy the armies of the living God? What is the reward for the man that kills this Philistine?" (1 Samuel 17:26). In these questions I don't hear ambition or youthful arrogance. I hear outrage! I hear David asking, "Why aren't you defending God, His honor, and His people? Why isn't anyone doing anything? Who's going to go fight?"

Is There *Not* a Cause?

David's questions probably felt like a not-so-subtle slap in the face for the unmoving masses that made up Saul's army. This might not have been true of all but it certainly was true of at least one—Eliab, David's oldest brother. Hearing David's questions, Eliab shredded his little brother: "Why are you here? Who's taking care of the sheep while you come up here to see what's going on? I know you, you arrogant little punk! You just want to see the battle!" Ouch, right? But watch David's reaction.

He doesn't get angry or get in Eliab's face. He doesn't defend himself. He only asks a question:

"Is there not a cause?" (1 Samuel 17:29 KJV)

When you volunteer for the fight, you have to know that you are going to deal with questions. They will question your motives and abilities. Some will question out of love and concern for you. Others will question out of envy. No matter what, listen to your heart, strengthen yourself in your faith and step into the battle anyway.

Life Lesson: God is less concerned with your abilities as a warrior than He is about your heart for the battle.

Who Are You Fighting For?

Who are you fighting for? This is the key question, and there are only three possible answers: For you, for your people, or for God.

For You

Those who fight for themselves fight *only* for themselves. It's an exercise in self-exaltation and selfishness. In reality, it's idolatry, but the image you worship isn't made of wood, stone, or precious metal. Instead the object of your worship is the image staring back at you in the mirror but the cause of self is too small to defeat the giant and so you will remain like the rest of the members of Israel's armies, hiding behind the rocks.

For Your People

Those who fight for their people appear to be noble. In fact, they appear to have the heart of a shepherd, but they don't. These are the people-pleasers and popularity-seekers. They don't want to win to protect God's people (the shepherd) but to win their favor. This is the way of the weak and insecure leader who is driven by the winds of popularity and the whims of the people. This is the kind of leader King Saul was. He disobeyed God because of his own selfishness and the selfishness of those who followed him (1 Samuel 15:13–23). The cause of popularity, which again is really self, is too small to win the victory against Goliath.

For God

The only way to win against insurmountable odds is to fight for a cause bigger than you. "David, who are you fighting for?" David's answer was, "I come to you [Goliath] in the name of the LORD of hosts, the God of the Armies of Israel" (1 Samuel 17:45).

When you are facing giants, you had better know why you are there. If you are ever going to risk it all, it will almost certainly be for a cause that is bigger than yourself. For a David, only God and His kingdom is a cause worthy of one's life.

Maybe you have heard the giant defying God and His armies. Let me promise you this: As you move toward the front lines, you will begin to hear the criticism of your motives and the questions of your abilities. Remember, abilities are amplified through God's anointing but only when our motives are pure and submitted to the Lord. The altar of self is too small to hold a giant. Only the altar of devotion to God can receive such a sacrifice.

Principle 3: A David has a heart for God.

He fights not for his own glory but the glory of the One who saved him, for God's people, and for His kingdom.

Where are the Davids?

CHAPTER 4

Heart of Faith

Stepping Out on the Promise

In Chapter 1 we discovered that worship is transformational because it allows you to see the Lord more clearly. What's cool is that when you really see Him, suddenly everything else looks a lot smaller. Because of this, worship is the door into truly walking by faith, so there is nothing more important than worship. It is from this perspective that light is separated from darkness, truth reveals the lie, and we begin to build our faith on eternal things instead of the temporary.

What God Sees

They say that everything is created twice: first in the mind of the creator, and then in the reality of his or her experience in time and space. Though this usually refers to the human creative experience, that is also how God operates. He sees and creates.

Life is the process, but you are the product. God uses the processes of life and maturity to bring His product (us) into being. Scripture says it like this: God declares the end, or the product, from the beginning.

> Remember the former things of old; for I am God, and there is no other; I am God, and there is none like me, *declaring the end from the beginning and from ancient times things not yet done*, saying, 'My counsel shall stand, and I will accomplish all my purpose.' (Isaiah 46:9–10)

Jesus was the Lamb slain before the foundation of the world (Revelation 13:8). That means that *before* there was a world, in God's mind He had already paid for humanity's sin. Wow! Think about that. Science dates the creation of the universe at several billion years ago, but in God's plan, His sacrifice that paid for our salvation existed before He set the first star in place. Jesus's crucifixion two thousand years ago was only the fulfillment of God's plan from eternity past. The Bible says it this way:

> But when the fullness of time had come, God sent forth his Son, born of woman, born under the law, to redeem those who were under the law, so that we might receive adoption as sons. (Galatians 4:4–5)

So in a very real way, time just caught up to God's plan for humanity, fulfilled in Jesus Christ! That's amazing, but what does that mean to you? It means that to God, you are already the man or woman who will fulfill the purposes for which you were created and that you will reign as His king or queen through that calling in His kingdom. You just need to catch up to the moment that becomes reality in your life.

Don't Despise the Day of Small Things

The prophet Zechariah says something incredible in the book that bears his name.

> Do not despise these small beginnings, for the LORD rejoices to see the work begin ... (Zechariah 4:10)

We live in a "microwave world," where everything is fast: fast food, high-speed internet, growth of knowledge, access to information, and everything else. We have jet airplanes that can take us to other continents in five hours and high-speed trains that can travel over two hundred miles an hour. Everything in this world is fast ... unless you are talking about God. If this is a "microwave world" then God's kingdom, and the development of His leaders, is much more of a "slow-cooker" process. This is a problem because too often we expect a promotion *today*. We get impatient about our calling. It's like, "Come on, God! Did you forget that You anointed me to be king? I want the throne. This [fill in the blank with your calling] needs leadership, and I'm the one You called for the job! I'm ready! Just let me loose!"

People often forget about David's life as a shepherd before he started slaying giants. Whatever romanticized thoughts you may have about shepherds, throw them out. In ancient Israel, nobody ever said, "When I grow up, I want to be a shepherd." On the socioeconomic spectrum, shepherds were at the bottom. They were loners who spent all their time around stinky, mindless animals that tended to get themselves either lost or eaten. Shepherds were not respected. They were not well educated. They didn't get invited to parties. Think about it; David didn't even get invited to stand before the prophet Samuel to be considered as the next king of Israel. He was a shepherd. Do you want to know what's worse? After David was anointed to become the next king of Israel, he still had to go back to the fields and watch sheep (1 Samuel 16:19).

> **Life Lesson:** It doesn't matter where you are. What matters is where you are going, so make the place you find yourself count by growing there.

Where you find yourself today is no indication of where God is going to lead you tomorrow. Of course, it helps to have the right last name, but that only gives you the connections to get in the door. After that, it's your anointing that will keep you there. Remember this clearly: *Only* God can lift up someone from the shepherd's field and place him or her in the palace. You see, it doesn't matter where you come from or even where you are. What matters is who God created you to be.

Though this is true, the next question is the most important if you are going to make your time in the pasture count:

What does God want you to learn while you're here?

David was sent back to the field. Why? Because the field had been David's university. It was in the field that David learned to worship and play his lyre. It was in the field that David learned to use a sling and a stone to kill lions and bears. It was in the field that David learned to care for sheep. When you look at it like that, in a very real way it was as a shepherd that David learned how to be king. Remember, God didn't want a king to rule over Israel. He wanted a shepherd to love and care for Israel, leading that nation into greater and greater dimensions of victory. That's why when they came to anoint David to be the king of Israel, they said, "In times past, when Saul was king over us, it was you who led out and brought in Israel. And the LORD said to you, 'You shall be shepherd of my people Israel, and you shall be prince over Israel'" (2 Samuel 5:2).

What's in Your Hand?

Where are you right now? What does God need you to learn while you are there? Wherever you are, God has you there on purpose. God is huge. His plan is beyond your wildest imaginations, and everything He's doing in your life is positioning you to get there. When you understand that, you will realize that He did not bring you here just to wait until your "real ministry" opens up. He brought you here today so you could learn skills that you will need to fulfill your created purpose tomorrow.

Your heart of faith sees the promise God has over your life and gains the daily victories necessary to get you there.

We know that David was no warrior, so how was David

prepared for his battle against the giant when he was a shepherd? I'm glad you asked. Listen to David's answer.

> But David said to Saul, "Your servant (David) used to keep sheep for his father. And when there came a lion, or a bear, and took a lamb from the flock, I went after him and struck him and delivered it out of his mouth. And if he arose against me, I caught him by his beard and struck him and killed him. Your servant has struck down both lions and bears, and this uncircumcised Philistine shall be like one of them, for he has defied the armies of the living God." And David said, "The LORD who delivered me from the paw of the lion and from the paw of the bear will deliver me from the hand of this Philistine." (1 Samuel 17:34–37)

On that fateful morning when David was to meet Goliath, he had already gained the skills needed to kill the giant. He didn't want to go into battle wearing Saul's armor, as if he was Saul's "Mini-Me." David wanted to fight the battle himself, with his sling and a few good stones because *that* sling had already defeated "giants."

> **Life Lesson:** You *need* to be you. God anointed/called you because He needs to use you, with all your unique talents ... and troubles. It's you He anointed. It's through you that He's going to win the victory so go and fight.

David had already killed lions and bears with the skills he had learned as a shepherd protecting sheep. He didn't need a special weapon to defeat the giant. David used what was in his hand, a tool that he had proven reliable on the battlefield of life. That is what he used to kill Goliath. In the same way, it is the skills you learn in your time as a "shepherd" that God will use when you step into your "reign as king" to fulfill your created purpose. Your victories today equip you for your victories tomorrow.

Principle 4: A David is a learner.

A David has the faith to understand that where he is today is designed by God to give him the skills he will need to bring the victories in the battles he will face tomorrow.

Where are the Davids?

SECTION 2

THE WILDERNESS

The Process That Proves A David

Many are called but few are chosen.

—Jesus in Matthew 22:14

Jesus, full of the Holy Spirit, left the Jordan and was led by the Spirit into the wilderness, where for forty days he was tempted by the devil.

...Jesus returned to Galilee (from the wilderness) in the power of the Spirit, and news about him spread through the whole countryside.

—Luke 4:1–2, 14

The wilderness is the place of proving because it is always your journey through the wilderness that creates the pathway to the throne. Though true, this is no simple avenue to meander along

29

on your way to reign. No. It is a place of darkness. It's the den of devils and the habitation of thieves, but more than that it also has always been the place of transition and transformation for the people of God throughout the ages. It is the place Abraham traveled to enter Promised Land. It is the where Jacob wrestled with God and became a prince named Israel. It is the place where Joseph was sold as a slave to become a prince in Egypt. It is the place where a slave people became a victorious nation. It is the place where Jesus faced Satan and his temptations, to return victoriously in the power of the Spirit. It is where, for the sake of our story, Jesus's ancestor David was driven by a madman to have his character proven before his ascent to the highest office on earth: king of Israel.

What is the wilderness? It is the place of trial. No great man or woman of God ever ascended to their places in the kingdom without first being tested in trial and tribulation. This is the toll that must be paid. Each of us is called by God, and so He equips us with the tools we need. Our part is simply this: We must pass through the trials of our wilderness ... victoriously. That is the difference-maker in the story of each of these men and nations mentioned above. Many have entered the wilderness but only those who continued on, serving God faithfully through to the other side, ever enter the place where they are entrusted to reign from the throne they were created to sit upon.

As you enter the wilderness, you must know that it is the place where your promise is placed in jeopardy. This is true of each of the great people of scripture and it will be true of you. Some through faith, have won in this place of testing, while others have lost. Whether it is Sarah being taken by Abemelech, Esau coming for Jacob with four hundred men, or the nation of Israel turning from the Promised Land to return to wander in the wilderness for forty years, each time it appears completely impossible for God's promise to ever come to pass. The fact is this: your right, and your calling won't be anything more than your fondest dream without your complete faith in one thing:

This is *not* your promise.
It's His.

Only God can do what He has said He will do. You can't bring it to pass, but you can prevent it. So what do you do? How do you win in the wilderness? You serve God faithfully in the midst of every doubt, fear, and tragedy that screams in our ears, "Your dream is *dead*!"

It is not dead. In fact, it is so close you could almost touch it. Just keep walking, following the One who gave the promise to you.

The wilderness is the place of proving so be proven *faithful*.

Where are the Davids?

CHAPTER 5

Goliath

The Looser of the King's Anointing

Looser: one who looses or releases

We have talked of Goliath for a couple of chapters, but I need to leave you with one more important fact—one that if you don't recognize it, you will never become a David. A David will always have a giant. That's just the way it is. If you don't want a fight, then you don't want the crown or the throne that goes with it. You may wonder why. You might even feel it's not fair, but it is what it is. Why? Because Goliath is the looser of the anointing.

You look at the giant. He's so huge that he looks like a hairy mountain with limbs. You hear his voice as he bellows out threats that promise your quick and painful end. He's so intimidating. Everything about him reeks of death, from the waves of stench rolling from his mouth to the odor of dried blood that seems to emanate from his very pores. The giant is a killing machine. He doesn't look like the looser of the anointing. He looks like death personified, but that's kind of the point.

You Are the Sacrifice

When the Lord told the prophet to anoint a son of Jesse to be the next king of Israel, Samuel asked how he could do that because Saul would kill him if he found out what he was doing. The Lord's answer was interesting. He said, "Tell Saul that you are going to Bethlehem to make a sacrifice." Did the God of the universe have to resort to lying to bring His will to pass? No, God didn't lie. Samuel was going to offer a sacrifice. It wasn't a wooly little lamb or even a heifer. No, the sacrifice was David.

Your anointing has one purpose: to keep God's people free to serve Him. Because of this, you are truly the servant of all. It's funny; when you get anointed to be king, your heart is filled with dreams of glory and conquest. That's because in the beginning, each of us thinks that the anointing is for us. We think, "It's because of how amazing I am. That's why I've been anointed to be king." The reality is this: You are the sacrifice. You are Jesus on the cross, dying to save everyone but Himself. That's why on His way to die on that tree, Jesus told His disciples, "Pick up your cross and follow me." Yes, you have a king's anointing, but it's not for you. It's for those you are called to fight for and rescue. You are the sacrifice.

Life Lesson: You are the sacrifice.

Let that sink in. Being "king" sounded so awesome when the oil was poured over your head and you heard the prophet's words as he laid his hands on you and declared, "Surely you are the Lord's anointed." You just didn't realize how much it would cost you. As you enter the battlefield, staring at the giant, you realize that by entering this fight you're dying to your hopes, your dreams, your life ... everything, but you need to remember why. God needs you to allow for His life to live in you so that you can fulfill His hopes and see His dreams come true. He dreams of bringing His kingdom into this world and seeing His people set free. That is why it costs so much. That is the price of leadership. That is why you were anointed to be A David.

What Looks Like the End of Your Life Is Really Just the Beginning

As you face the giant, you need to know this one thing: Goliath has arrived only to catapult you into your destiny. He thinks he's going to make you like so many other of his victims, but he doesn't know that he's never faced anyone like you before.

It's true that the historical Goliath whom David fought in the valley that day was huge, but the legend of Goliath was even bigger. It had even reached the ears of Israel's King Saul, who warned David of this man's killing gift.

The giant you face will be huge too, but in the same way, he's *not* as big as he sounds. The enemy (Satan, the devil, or one of his stooges) is a talker. His attack is always first in your mind, and

35

he is never as deadly as he has said he is. Goliath said to David, "After I'm done tearing you to pieces, I'm going to feed what's left of your body to the birds and beasts! There won't be enough to bury!" He wants to intimidate you. He needs you to believe that he's going to win because if he can convince you of that, he will. He is a giant. He is your enemy. He is there to kill you, but as you face him on the battlefield, you need to know only one thing: You are *destined to win*!

God has called you and anointed you to be His king, but the reality is this: You, my little friend, are nothing but a shepherd. You will never reign as long as you remain in the comfortable confines of the pasture. The battle—in fact, *this* battle—is the only thing that could ever raise you from obscurity to be considered worthy of the throne. You are here, but you must realize that you are here on purpose. When God anointed you to be a king, He anointed you to be the champion of His people. You have been anointed for warfare. Look what God says about His servant David in battle:

> I have found David my servant;
> with my sacred oil I have anointed him.
> My hand will sustain him;
> surely my arm will strengthen him.
> The enemy will not get the better of him;
> the wicked will not oppress him.
> I will crush his foes before him
> and strike down his adversaries.
> My faithful love will be with him,

and through my name his horn will be exalted.
(Psalm 89:20–24)

Check this out! The giant showed up thinking that he was there to win the victory for his people, but God brought him there to show the world that no enemy, no matter how big, can stand against A David. Why? Because God fights for His Davids. Goliath thought he showed up to win, but he only showed up to show off the next king. He showed up to loose David's anointing.

Life Lesson: The giant/Goliath is the looser of the anointing.

Here's the one bit of bad news: This battle is just the beginning. Goliath is only the first giant of the first battle. More are coming. None will ever be as large as Goliath, but that doesn't mean that the battles will get easier. In many ways, Goliath will be your easiest victory. As you face the other giants of betrayal and loss, always remember that you are destined for victory. Why? Because you are A David, and because of that, your God fights for you Himself.

Principle 5: A David's anointing can be loosed only through battle.

A David is anointed to reign through battle, but because of that, the king's anointing can only be loosed through battle. Do not fear the giant. Go out and conquer him through the power of God's mighty hand, moving through you.

Caveat: Be careful when you slay another man's giant.

Saul was the king of Israel. As a king in the ancient world, Saul was Israel's champion, and so it was expected that Saul would lead his people in battle. That is what kings did but not in this battle. As Goliath taunted God and His people, Saul sat quietly upon his throne. Remember, the altar of self cannot receive the sacrifice of self but only the sacrifice of others. Saul was happy to allow David to fight Goliath. If he lost, it would prove that the giant was too big to defeat. If he won, Saul would take the credit for the foresight of allowing this young warrior to fight. Unfortunately, Saul forgot one important fact:

In the eyes of the people, Goliath was *his* giant to kill.

When David killed Goliath, the women of Israel began to sing, "Saul has killed his thousands but David has killed his ten thousands" (1 Samuel 18:7). In allowing David to kill his giant, Saul had lost the #1 spot in the affections of his people. And so this is where it began. Out of jealousy, Saul began to hate David. He hated David because the people loved him. He hated David because he saw God's favor on him. He hated David because in his heart, he knew that he was destined to be the next king of Israel. This is all true, but ultimately Saul hated David for one reason and one reason alone. He hated David because he allowed David to defeat his giant.

Life Lesson: Never let anyone else defeat your giants.

You may be scared and may recognize that it's impossible to win, but go out and fight anyway! Step out on the battlefield for the glory of the Lord your God, His kingdom, and His people. Swing your sword, and allow God to win the victory through your hand. Remember you will always miss 100% of the shots you never take. Take the shot!

Where are the Davids?

CHAPTER 6

Jonathans

And the People You Lose along the Way

After David had finished talking with Saul, Jonathan became one in spirit with David, and he loved him as himself. From that day Saul kept David with him and did not let him return home to his family. And Jonathan made a covenant with David because he loved him as himself. Jonathan took off the robe he was wearing and gave it to David, along with his tunic, and even his sword, his bow and his belt.

—1 Samuel 18:1–4

In the Bible, Jonathan is a man torn between two kings. He was David's best friend, but Jonathan was also King Saul's firstborn son and next in line for the throne. Torn between allegiances to his father and his best friend, Jonathan ends up a casualty of his father's selfish ambition to continue his legacy, and in one day both father and son died on the same battlefield.

If you are like most Davids, you may feel that people are always leaving your life. As if through a turnstile on the subway, people often come into your life in a flash and then are gone as quickly as they arrived. So many times you may wonder, "Why? Is something wrong with me? Why does everyone I love seems to leave?" The reality of the life of a David is that you are going to lose people along the way as you walk with Jesus. There are a few reasons for that, but just remember one thing:

God is taking you somewhere.

Everything that He brings into your life is to guide you to your destiny in Him. Your relationships are part of that molding. People can choose paths contrary to God and His will, and they often do, but He will play the cards He's been dealt to bring you to where you were created to be, if you stay faithful to Him.

Three People You Lose along the Way

Fathers, the People You Have Served, Admired, and Loved

The relationship between Saul and David is one of the most complex in scripture. Saul loved David, and David loved Saul, but Saul tried to kill David. This love became clear in their two meetings after David fled from Jerusalem to save his life from the king's jealous rage.

> When David finished saying this, Saul asked, "Is
> that your voice, David my son?" And he wept
> aloud. (1 Samuel 24:16)

Saul loved David. David had faithfully served Saul. In fact, David's music had been Saul's only peace in times of great demonic torment (1 Samuel 16:23). David had been Saul's armor bearer (1 Samuel 16:21). Most important, David won victories that Saul could not. As long as Saul felt relatively secure in the throne, he allowed David to thrive and win victories, but once he realized that David was created to rule Israel, that all changed. From that point on, he tried relentlessly to kill David.

If you are a David, you will have "Sauls." Sauls are fearful of so many things. They are fearful of your anointing. They are fearful of losing their throne (position). They are fearful of losing the opportunity for legacy through nepotistic succession. Sauls keep you down, suppressing your opportunities because they fear your success. At times, they send you to do a job that they know they can't do for the purpose of advancing their kingdoms. When you come back triumphantly, they quickly send you back to your corner and take credit for your accomplishments ... that is, until you can't be hidden any longer.

As your fame grows so does the threat to Saul's security and throne. After a while he begins to throw javelins. Confused, you make excuses for him, saying it was unintentional or that something was "misunderstood" but soon, you realize that you're the only one who misunderstands. Saul is trying to kill you. This is both terrifying and deeply saddening. You have loved and served this man. You have risked your own life and future to protect and advance his kingdom.

Through the hurt of betrayal and the deep wound it leaves, you know one thing: You need to let Saul go.

Letting Saul go can take many different forms. You might need to set new boundaries for the relationship. You may need to disassociate from him socially. Sometimes you may have to run somewhere where you can be safe from thrown javelins. Whatever it looks like, this is not something done quickly or in the heat of the moment. The people in your life aren't always throwing javelins when they hurt you. There will be times when you will need correction and redirection. That is part of growing into spiritual maturity. Your anointing doesn't give you all the answers. Be patient. Find the heart of the person you are serving, and determine whether that person is for you or against you. If they are for you, submit and grow spiritually but if they are against you, you may need to run for your life. Just be sure you know which side of the fence they are really on. It was only after a long time of increasingly obvious attempts on his life that David determined he had to leave Saul's court.

Life Lesson: Leave the bitterness in Saul's Court

There is a portion of the human soul that cries out for justice. It is part of the image of God in each of us. That cry for justice, though right, must be left behind. We must forgive, as David forgave, if we are to ascend into our kingdom assignment, as he did. How do I know David forgave Saul? Because he didn't kill him. David had two clear opportunities to kill Saul, but he never touched him. Even after all that Saul had done to David, when David learned that the king was dead, he tore his clothes and mourned for him (2 Samuel 1:11–12).

If you allow your hurt to become bitterness, you will abort the character that God is trying to shape in you through these experiences. Remember you are in the wilderness. God is shaping your character through the process of trial. Don't let the enemy steal your victory. Forgive, and allow God to shape your life to reflect His. How? Don't talk about Saul; pray for him. Don't plead your case; plead for God to make you a leader who will never hurt the next generation of Davids as it rises into greatness.

"Vengeance is mine, declares the Lord" (Deuteronomy 32:35). That means it's not yours. Leave the Sauls to their own fears, trying to protect their own kingdoms. If they are not careful, they will fall on their own swords. Your job is to become someone after God's own heart. That means you need to forgive and leave bitterness behind.

Fans, the People Who Fall in Love with You from Afar

Michal was like every other single woman in the kingdom. She was smitten by this young rock-star warrior with the tanned face and muscular physique. David was every young lady's dream. Being the daughter of King Saul, Michal was close enough that she could almost touch him … and then he became her husband. It was the fantasy life! She was the wife of the rock star. It was perfect—at least until Daddy wanted him dead. Hard times have a way of separating the people who are jockeying for position in the adoring crowd from those who are committed to walk through the darkness with you. While they were separated, as her husband ran for his life, Michal's commitment seemed to wane. Did she believe her father's accusations against her husband? Doubtful. She had her brother Jonathan there to remind her of David's devotion to Saul and of her father's jealousy over the affections of the people. No matter the reason, Michal became the second of David's losses, and she was married to another man (1 Samuel 25:44).

Though the marriage technically was restored (2 Samuel 3:13–16), Michal was never the same toward David. She seemed distant and even mocked David as he worshipped the Lord (2 Samuel 6:20–23). Though the result was a broken relationship with David, Michal's biggest issue was her lack of relationship with God. The deepest levels of intimacy two people can share are only possible when each of them has God as *the* love in their lives. If that had been the case, Michal's reaction to David's worship of God would have been joy and admiration instead of embarrassment and disdain. Her criticism created a distance between them that was never overcome. It seems that from that point forward Michal was never again united with David sexually and died childless.

Life Lesson: Don't mistake your fans for your friends.

Fans fall in love with what you do, NOT with who you are. They may be enamored with your talents or infatuated with your gifts, but they lack real commitment to you.

How do we navigate life to know the difference between fans

and friends? Here, Jesus is our guide. The Gospel of John answers this question.

> Now while he was in Jerusalem at the Passover Festival, many people saw the signs he was performing and believed in his name. But Jesus would not entrust himself to them, for he knew all people. He did not need any testimony about mankind, for he knew what was in each person. (John 2:23–25)

There are two main points here:

1. Don't just give yourself to people too quickly. People get excited about achievements and are enamored with personalities. That does not mean they care about you. Let people prove themselves faithful to you before you share the depths of your heart with them.

2. Understand that people are people, and most want to use you to help them reach their goals. This is selfishness, and it's the root and product of every sin from Eden until now. You will need ambitious people to join your team as you seek to fulfill your destiny, but realize that not all those who walk with you are linked to you. Only those truly committed to you will stay through the dark days while all the pretenders pack their things and leave.

Friends, the People Who Truly Love You More than Their Own Lives

As I mentioned in the beginning of this chapter, Jonathan was a man torn between two kings—torn between allegiance to his father and his best friend. In the end, Jonathan became a casualty of Saul's selfish ambition, dying on the same battlefield as his father. So how could Jonathan possibly give up, not only the throne but in the end, his life for David? Simple: Jonathan loved David. Jesus said, "Greater love has no one than this, that someone lay down his life for his friends." (John 15.:13) This is the kind of love Jonathan had for David.

The "Jonathans" in your life will love you, maybe even more than you love them. Though some have tried to make David and Jonathan's relationship something that it was not, these two men clearly and truly loved each other. It definitely seems, however, that as much as David loved Jonathan, Jonathan loved David more. Pure love produces pure desires. Jonathan's love for David was a love that desired the best for David and the best for God's people. That pure love for David was, in many ways, at the expense of what was best for himself. Pure love is the love of self-sacrifice. It is a love that sacrifices self for another. This is the rarest form of friendship, yet if you are going to be a David, you will lose a Jonathan.

We lose our Jonathans to tragedy. There is no other way. Anything short of this, the love of these friends would survive, but tragedy creates a chasm that cannot be crossed. Whether that tragedy is sickness and disease or the tests and trials of life, the result is always the same: You lose one of the most important people in your life.

Life Lesson: You will only ever have two kinds of people in your life:

1. Those who want *from* you (Sauls, fans, and everyone else)
2. Those who want *for* you (friends)

The Why

If you are A David, you might have already lost more than you ever dreamed you would, or you might have not lost anyone yet. Regardless of where you find yourself, your question is probably the same: "Why does it have to be this way?" One of my Jonathans once said to me, "Some relationships are only meant to last for a time (season). You need to let those go. Always remember God will never remove a relationship that you need to fulfill your destiny."

God knows what you need to help shape you to become the person you were created to be. God brings people into your life for a time and a purpose that you may not understand. You had to have them in your life, but losing them hurts. They're not just God's tools to shape you; they are people that God brings into your life so you can love and enjoy the ride together, even if only for a little while. For that time, these people serve you in three ways:

- To protect you
- To bring you into places/opportunities
- To mature and purify you

These three people mentioned in this chapter affect each of these aspects in your life at different times but Fathers generally bring new opportunities. Saul invited David to the palace as a musician and later allowed him to fight Goliath, propelling him into the national spotlight. Friends protect us, as Jonathan protected David, warning him of his father's murderous intentions. Fans, like Michal, bring us to reality as we realize that most love what we do, not who we are. All three act to bring A David to new levels of purity and maturity.

As you suffer the pain of the loss of these people through betrayal or other events, it's important to remember that God will use this pain to bring purity to your heart and to your motives. The throne to which you are called requires a purity that isn't natural. It only comes through suffering. Paul says something crazy in the Letter to the Philippians that only becomes clear after you read it through the lens of that last sentence: "I want to know Christ—yes, to know the power of his resurrection and participation in his sufferings, becoming like him in his death" (Philippians 3:10).

All of us want God's power, His reign, His might but none of us wants Jesus's sufferings. If you are going to become A David, like Paul became, then you must participate in His sufferings because you can't have one without the other.

As we get ready to wrap up this chapter you need to realize that no matter of how these people may have hurt him, David loved each of them. In fact, it was because He loved them that these people had such a big effect on David. This chapter is not about holding yourself back from these relationships. It's about embracing them. You need to love and love deeply to allow for the richness of these relationships to become shaping elements in your life. Those that you need for your destiny will remain while the others will be listed as those you lost along the way.

Principle 6: A David's life is often filled with the losses of those he loved most, like Jonathan.

A David is a person of deep passion, linked and given in relationships with others. He loves and is loyal, even when others may not deserve this loyalty. Above all, A David chooses to allow himself to love truly and give himself truly so that the fullness of life's greatest treasure of true friendship can shape his soul. If that person leaves and the pain comes, it is *because* he loved. God will use this pain to grow A David and prepare him to sit on the throne of his calling to reign for Him.

Where are the Davids?

CHAPTER 7

Ziklag

The Journey from Refuge to Reign

As a David, you are going to walk through the Valley of the Shadow of Death. It's called the wilderness, and you have to go through it to enter into your promise. This wilderness is God's process of development. Because of that, the wilderness is a place of hardship and fear. For an ancient Israelite, the wilderness was a terrifying place where demons lived and marauders raided. You live exposed here. Because of that there is little rest and little comfort in the wilderness. During David's time in the wilderness, he found rest in only two places: in the presence of his friends and in the city of Ziklag. Before David began his reign, both of these comforts were nearly stolen from him when he faced his Kairos Moment.

Friends

> David left Gath and escaped to the cave of
> Adullam. When his brothers and his father's
> household heard about it, they went down to
> him there. All those who were in distress or in
> debt or discontented gathered around him, and
> he became their commander. About four hundred
> men were with him. (1 Samuel 22:1–2)

Running for his life, David escaped from Saul into the
wilderness. He was desperate for safety. How desperate was he?
Desperate enough to walk into Goliath's hometown carrying
the giant's sword as his only weapon to ask for help. Of course
that didn't go well, and David ended up living alone in a cave.
That might have been the end of it, but people began to hear
of the state of Israel's greatest champion. Soon, news spread—
"David is hiding in the Cave of Adullam." It was at that point
that something amazing happened; men started coming. Not
the courtly crowd of kingly balls or royal processions but the
discontented, the distressed, and the debtors. This was no army.
At best it was a ragtag band of social misfits, but this was who
came, and other than David's own family, they were the only
ones who did.

Life Lesson: True friends are hard to find.

It often is in the darkness of your isolation that you will gain
your closest friends. These friends are often very different from

many others you may have had before. These are the friends who will walk with you in both your darkest moments and your greatest achievements. It's easy to be friends when you're standing victoriously on the chest of Goliath or when you are invited to the palace of the king. It is quite another thing to be friends when you are running for your life, but it's there that you find out who will stand with you until the end. These are the people who don't chant your name because of your most recent victories but who love you because of all you have been through together. These are the warriors who will become your "Mighty Men." They represent some of God's greatest gifts to you and will become your greatest gifts to the world.

Ziklag

> So on that day Achish gave him Ziklag, and it has belonged to the kings of Judah ever since. David lived in Philistine territory a year and four months. (1 Samuel 27:6–7)

Ziklag wasn't much—just a little village on the outskirts of the kingdom of Philistia. The Philistine king gave it to David as a refuge, but it became home for him, his men, and all of their families. *Home* is a rare thing in the wilderness. In fact, it's so rare, it has to be a gift. Why? Because the wilderness is *not* where you are called to live. The wilderness isn't your home. You are just passing through. The wilderness is the pathway to promise—nothing more but also nothing less. Oh, but it's *so nice* to have a place to rest in your wilderness. Just having a place to lay your head on your pillow in your bed … man, there's nothing like it. To have a place where your wife and children can play and laugh means all the world to you when all that remains of what was a promising future are the flickering embers of the dream you once believed came from God. Of course, you are still serving God and His people as best as you can. You raid the raiders, defending Israel's defenseless masses, who should be guarded by Saul, their king. Yes, he's the one who's trying to kill you, but that doesn't matter. These are God's people. They are your people! No matter who sits on the throne, these are your people, and your calling is to serve them, whether you have a position or not. Then suddenly it happens. When returning from one of these rides, David saw it. Smoke rising from near … *No!* It couldn't be … Ziklag!

David and his men reached Ziklag on the third day. Now the Amalekites had raided the Negev and Ziklag. They had attacked Ziklag and burned it, and had taken captive the women and everyone else in it, both young and old. They killed none of them, but carried them off as they went on their way. When David and his men reached Ziklag, they found it destroyed by fire and their wives and sons and daughters taken captive. So David and his men wept aloud until they had no strength left to weep. David's two wives had been captured— Ahinoam of Jezreel and Abigail, the widow of Nabal of Carmel. David was greatly distressed

because the men were talking of stoning him;
each one was bitter in spirit because of his sons
and daughters. But David found strength in the
Lord his God. (1 Samuel 30:1–6)

I don't think words can adequately describe how David and his men felt in that moment. Their homes were destroyed; their wives and children were taken to be slaves or worse; the little bit of goods they had in the world were stolen. Wasn't it bad enough that they were exiles from their homeland, living among pagans who did not know God? Now they truly had nothing. Is it any wonder that David's men—his partners in this dark journey—thought about stoning him? But then a most amazing thing happened. In the midst of the chaos, David did something that every David must learn to do: He looked up.

He had to face the reality that everything he had was gone. The evidence of that truth was all around him, so he had to look up. He looked to the One who is truth and found his strength in his God. David put himself in a place to hear, not the murmuring of his stone-gathering men, but the voice of the Lord.

Then David said to Abiathar the priest, the son
of Ahimelek, "Bring me the ephod." Abiathar
brought it to him, and David inquired of the
Lord, "Shall I pursue this raiding party? Will I
overtake them?" "Pursue them," he answered.
"You will certainly overtake them and succeed in
the rescue." (1 Samuel 30:7–8)

The rest of the story? "David recovered all …" (1 Samuel 30:18). That means David and his men got everything back. Their wives, their children, their donkeys and camels, they all came home.

Life Lesson: It is how you respond in the
Kairos Moment that matters most.

How you respond in your moments of crisis reveal the most about who you are—or rather, who you have become. This inner man/woman who is revealed in what I call *Kairos Moments* truly determines your destination in life. A Kairos Moment is the intersection where the eternal purposes/promises/plans of God meets one of His children on the plane of time. In biblical Greek, the word Kairos means "appointed time or season." In my understanding the Kairos Moment is the final exam. It is literally the door you must walk through to enter God's promise in your life and because of that, it is usually the hardest test you have ever faced. I mean, it should be. The Kairos Moment fundamentally changes the course of a person's history and sometimes world history. In the life of David, this is one of those moments. David had a choice. He could have joined his men in damning their circumstances. He could have lamented all that he had lost and just rolled over, allowing his men to throw stone upon stone at him until breath left his body. In some ways, that must have been at least a little tempting. At least then this misery finally would have ended and maybe he could have found some peace. But that's not what David did. He did what everyone must do if they are going to successfully move through their Kairos Moment.

He anchored himself in his faith and asked God, "What should I do?" God said, "Go! Overtake them! Don't stop until you get everything back that was stolen from you."

How different would David's story have been if he hadn't asked for God's direction in his Kairos Moment? There is one important lesson here that must be captured:

God uses life's most difficult moments, Kairos Moments, to launch His leaders into new dimensions of His promises. Why? Because in your conquest in that moment, your faith opens the door for you to live in that new dimension of promise.

Whether or not you ever reach the heights you dream of within your calling is determined by how you respond in crisis. Do you cower in the chaos or step into the storm by your faith in the One who called you? This is your Kairos Moment, and if you pass this test faithfully, it will open the door to God's promise and destiny for your life. Be faithful because you never know when you have passed the test. David didn't. David was just faithful and did what the Lord told him to do, but the next thing we read is that David—immediately after he recaptured all that was lost at Ziklag—was anointed to be the king over the tribe of Judah. Your destiny always follows your Ziklag if you will just follow your King.

Principle 7: A David has deep faith in God and that faith makes anything possible.

A David does not allow the circumstances of life to cloud his view of his God. He looks to God and finds the divine path that He has set before him, not only through the chaos but into destiny. A David is faithful in the tests and trials of this life, and through that faithfulness he recovers all that was lost, including his dreams.

Where are the Davids?

SECTION 3

REIGN

The throne is the fulfillment of the promise of God over the life of His child. This is what you have been waiting for and dreaming of ever since God first spoke it over your life—but it's not what you might expect. *This* is what you were made for. That is real. You feel it in every bone in your body. You sit back and smile, savoring the moment. You whisper the words, "I've finally made it." It's been a long road. It has cost you more than anyone will ever know, but all that you have been through has prepared you for this moment.

Many will envy your newfound position, but that's only because they don't understand. Most people look at the throne and see only its glory. Before being enthroned, we dream of the day when we will enter into all the promises that God ever gave us, but we must remember that the throne only puts us in position to do what we have been called to do.

The Throne and the Cross

What few know before they sit in their positional calling in the kingdom, that despite its glamor, the throne is really a place of sacrifice. Jesus said that He came to serve, not to be served. Later, He told His disciples that Christian leadership was not like leadership in the world's system. Those who are the greatest in the world are served by everyone beneath them, but in God's kingdom, "the greatest people" are the servants of all (Matthew 20:26; Mark 9:35). The throne is not a place where you are glorified. It is only a vehicle for God to raise up someone who will serve His people as He intended. You see, the only reason to have leaders in God's kingdom is because people need to be led to God:

- Moses was called to be a deliverer to bring Israel out of slavery and into the Promised Land that God had given Abraham.
- Elijah was called to be a prophet to bring Israel back to God.
- David was called to be king because Israel needed a shepherd.

The throne is not about your glory; it's about His. Your throne is God's invitation to become part of His story and the story of His people. Great men and women have been shipwrecked because they entered the position of their reign, due to either talent or nepotism, before they had the strength of character to support it. The throne comes with a crown, and that crown is heavy. If you have not developed the strength of character to support the crown, its weight can crush you. That's why the wilderness is not optional. If you are going to be A David, your motives must be refined in the fires of trial and tribulation, which can only come in the wilderness. Why? Because you can only enter your true calling when God knows that you are His and that you are so submitted to His will that it's not really *you* sitting on the throne; *He* is. You see, the thing that got you anointed the first time is the same thing that gets you anointed the second time and third time. It's your worship of the One you love. You're here because in your heart, it's about Him, not you.

Where are the Davids?

CHAPTER 8

Hebron

And David brought up his men who were with him, everyone with his household, and they lived in the towns of Hebron. And the men of Judah came, and there they anointed David king over the house of Judah ...

—2 Samuel 2:3–4

Hebron

Hebron is an interesting place. As the highest point in Israel and nineteen miles south of Jerusalem, the city of Hebron is perched high in the Judean Mountains, 3,050 feet above sea level. This city and its surrounding region have a unique and storied history. Hebron was one of the places Moses's twelve spies passed through while they surveyed the Promised Land, right before they epically failed to trust God and His promises, resulting in their forty-year hike around Mount Sinai.

Hebron was Caleb's home. He was one of only two faithful spies of the twelve mentioned above, and because of his faith, God promised him Hebron. That faith is illustrated perfectly by Caleb's famous words, "Now give me this mountain" (Joshua 14:12). There was just one problem. "This mountain" was the home of giants. Caleb didn't care. He stood on the words of God's promise through Moses: "On that day Moses swore to me, 'The land on which your feet have walked will be your inheritance and that of your children forever, because you have followed the Lord my God wholeheartedly'" (Joshua 14:9).

Hebron was the place where dreams came true. Even before the story of Caleb, Hebron was a central location in the story of God and His people. It was where Abraham finally settled in Canaan after separating from Lot (Genesis 13). It was in Hebron that the Lord told Abraham, "Look around from where you are … All the land that you see I will give to you and your offspring forever … Go, walk through the length and breadth of the land, for I am giving it to you" (Genesis 13:14–17). It was in Hebron that Abraham built his first altar in the Promised Land. It also is the location of the Cave of the Patriarchs, the ancient burial place of Abraham, Issac, and Jacob. During Abraham's lifetime, this cave would be his only permanent possession in the land that God had promised him. Hebron is then the place where God's promise finally becomes reality.

All of this history of Hebron is important because *this* is also the place where David was anointed the king of Judah.

The Place Where You Are Enthroned

Hebron is the place where God begins to fulfill the promise in the life of A David. It is not the end. It is only the first of the anointings of reign that God has designed to bring to David's life, but it is *not* David's first anointing. He was anointed as the king of Israel by the prophet Samuel when he was about seventeen (1 Samuel 16). Imagine—David was anointed king roughly thirteen years before he sat on his first throne, and even that was not the throne he was promised. Hebron was only the first stop in God's fulfillment of the promise in David. The road to Hebron was paved by David's faithfulness to God in the wilderness.

Whether it was Caleb, Abraham, or David, the key that unlocked Hebron was faithfulness. It was after Caleb refused to doubt God and after forty years of faithfully waiting in the wilderness that the door to enter his promise opened. It was when Abraham finally obeyed God and left all of his family, including Lot, that he settled in Hebron. It was the same with David. David was faithful—from being a shepherd anointed to be king to the mighty warrior who led Israel to victory; from becoming the son-in-law to the king to sparing that same king's life while he was trying to kill David. David was faithful through it all. Why was he crowned here? Because Hebron is the destination of faithfulness. David's faithfullness to God, combined with God's faithfulness to his promises, got him there. Hebron is the place where God's promise becomes realty.

Life Lesson: Faithfulness to God is only maintained through a deep relationship with God.

There are two primary elements in faithfulness to God:

1. Doing right through obedience to His Word
2. Being right through relationship with Him

The meaning of the name *Hebron* is interesting. It means company, association, community, or alliance. The word *Hebron* is literally a reflection of deep relationship ... the kind of relationship that binds people together and makes them committed partners throughout life. A David will arrive at Hebron to be enthroned only after growing into a deep and faithful relationship with God. The reason is simple: trust. David is a king, and kings reign. In God's kingdom, He establishes a king not because He wants to give someone power but because He has people who need leaders to take them to their destinies. We don't reign for ourselves. We reign for others. This is important because God will only enthrone a king that He reigns in.

Life Lesson: God will only enthrone the person He reigns in

Life Lesson: "Come with me to sacrifice."

I alluded to this in an earlier chapter but it needs repeating. In 1 Samuel 16:2–3, the prophet told King Saul that he was going to sacrifice to the Lord in Bethlehem. This wasn't a lie. Samuel was offering sacrifice, but it was not just the heifer; it was the future king. Reigning for God in our place in the kingdom is sacrifice. At times, it may look to the outsider like having authority and limelight, but it is a life lived to serve others. Jesus said that when much is given, much is required (Luke 12:48). For one to truly enter Hebron—not to be placed in a role by human nepotism but to truly enter to reign for God in His kingdom—you must live a life of sacrifice to God and for others. God will not set a man to reign over His people until He reigns within the heart of the man He has called to the throne. Why? Because God wants shepherds for His people, not rulers seeking power for themselves.

Please don't miss this. The biblical picture given to us in Hebron is that relationship is the place where the rule and reign of our ministries are established. The same thing that got you anointed is what gets you (finally) on the throne. It is your worship of God and submission to Him that enables you to truly serve Him from the throne.

The Third Anointing

Hebron is the place of David's first anointing to reign (2 Samuel 2:4), but it is also the place of his final anointing.

> When all the elders of Israel had come to King
> David at Hebron, the king made a covenant with
> them at Hebron before the Lord, and they anointed
> David king over Israel. (1 Samuel 5:3)

You need to understand this one point: You *never* get past *this place*. God can take you no higher than the highest point. You may get better titles; you may sit in different offices, but the thing that gets you into each of those places never changes. As I heard a great man of God once say, "The challenge is to keep the main thing the main thing." If you do, you can lead God's people to heights they never would have dreamed possible, but it never gets any more complicated than keeping your heart of worship to God. In other words, what got you anointed to become king at seventeen is what got you anointed as king at thirty and what will keep you anointed to reign for the rest of your life.

Life Lesson: You need permission to lead.

It is important to realize that you can only lead those who give you permission to lead them. I have seen people try all manner of strategies to get or even make people follow them. Usually, these are positional leaders who have not yet been given God's invitation to enter Hebron. Sadly, many of these people have destroyed their ministries and often several other people as they tried to keep people following them, just as King Saul did before them. In both of David's anointings to reign, the people asked him to lead them.

A David never needs to manipulate to maintain power. People follow A David because he follows after God. Lead those who will follow you, and do not concern yourself with those who won't. The Lord knows where He's leading you, and He knows who you'll need to have on your team when you get there.

Principle 8: A David is enthroned in the place where he enthroned God... in relationship with Him.

Hebron's foundations were laid in the heart of A David and were fortified in the trials of the wilderness. Thus, it is only after passing through these two formative elements that God invites you to realize the promise that has been in you since before you were born. It is hard to get there, but oh ... the view is so amazing at the place God created you to live.

Where are the Davids?

CHAPTER 9

Bathsheba

Passion or Passions

In the history of the world there has never been a great leader, regardless of the sphere of influence, who was not passionate. Passion is the greatest strength of any great leader but especially A David. It's this passion that makes a true worshipper, someone not satisfied just worshipping in church on Sunday but one who pursues God every day. King David was not satisfied with traditional worship. He pitched a tent in the backyard and created a new dimension of worship that brought the Ark of God's presence to Jerusalem so that he could be close to Him.

This is the same inner force that propels you onto the battlefield to defend God's people and face the giant. It is this passion that makes others want to follow you into the battle, knowing that they will face only what you have already conquered because you always lead from the front. Passion is your greatest strength. It is what makes you A David. It is also your greatest weakness.

What most people don't recognize is that all great strengths are also great weaknesses. That may seem untrue until you really think about it. To a hammer, every problem is a nail, which is great, unless it's a screw. In David's life, his passion was his guide. It is what led to some of the greatest stories in history, yet there comes a time in the life of A David when he must determine which passion must be followed and which must be set aside. A David must determine whether he will follow his passion or his passions.

David's passion for God was extraordinary. In Psalms, David's passion for God and His Word is everywhere:

I love you, LORD, my strength. (Psalm 18:1)

I will give thanks to the LORD with all my heart; I will tell of all Your wonders. (Psalm 9:1)

I keep my eyes always on the LORD. With him at my right hand, I will not be shaken. (Psalm 16:8)

The LORD is my light and my salvation-- whom shall I fear? The LORD is the stronghold of my life-- of whom shall I be afraid? (Psalm 27:1)

One thing I ask from the LORD, this only do I seek: that I may dwell in the house of the LORD all the days of my life, to gaze on the beauty of the LORD and to seek him in his temple. (Psalm 27:4)

> For great is your love, higher than the heavens;
> your faithfulness reaches to the skies. (Psalm
> 108:4)

> I long to dwell in your tent forever and take refuge
> in the shelter of your wings. (Psalm 61:4)

In these words you can hear the echo of a love and passion for God that is rare, yet there came a day when David chose to rest from his responsibilities as God's king over His people. The Bible tells us that it was spring, the time when kings go off to war, but David lingered at the palace (2 Samuel 11:1) and instead chose to look over his kingdom from his housetop. It was then that it happened; he caught a glimpse of something. He moved to get a better view, and suddenly he saw her—a beautiful young woman, bathing in the privacy of her rooftop. She had confidence in knowing that no building was so high that she would be seen and her immodesty revealed. Only from the heights of the palace could anyone see anything, and everyone knew that the king was at war with his men. But David wasn't at war. He was on his rooftop, staring, desiring, lusting, and making a decision. Would he turn his eyes and go inside, or would he linger and allow for his passion for this woman to grow? David had a choice. Would he continue to pursue his true passion, or would he be swayed by temptation and follow his base passions? David did choose, and his decision would change his family forever.

Life Lesson: You have to choose today how you will respond to the moral temptation that is coming tomorrow.

Passion or Passions

People have lots of passions. You can be passionate about your favorite team or about dance or about almost anything, but ultimately, you have only *one true* passion. Your *passion* sets the direction of your heart. Because of this, for a David, your supreme passion will always be aligned with your purpose. Passions, on the other hand, satisfy your selfishness (even if they are not sin). On this fateful night, David chose to follow his passions, and it brought tragedy to his family and heartbreak to his soul.

By the time it was over Amnon and Absalom, two of his oldest sons were dead, and his beautiful daughter Tamar had been raped and disgraced to the point that she would never marry or have children. Why? Because David chose to satisfy his passions rather than be faithful to his God.

Are You for Sale?

The questions that follow will change your life, if you let them. These are the questions every David needs to ask.

What do you value?

What do you stand for?

What matters more to you than anything else?

The answers to these questions will bring you needed clarity. They help you focus on what matters most and let you see their value to you.

But there's one more question, and this one may be the most important of all.

Are you for sale?

The question is, simply, are you able to be pulled away from the things you hold most dear? Are the values you hold able to be wrestled away from your grasp when (*not* if) the opportunity comes for compromise?

I ask these things for one simple reason; Satan will pay any price for a king's anointing.

Life Lesson: Satan will pay any price for a king's anointing.

Bathsheba was stunning, I'm sure. The king could have had any unmarried woman in the kingdom that he wanted, but Bathsheba wasn't an unmarried woman. In fact, her husband, Uriah, was listed as one of David's Mighty Men, but that didn't matter. David wanted *her*. How bad? Bad enough that he allowed for his passions for her to overwhelm his love for God, his people, and his friend. The die was cast, and the decision was made. But, my fellow David, if King David had known the price he would pay for his lusts, he would have run from the rooftop, never to return.

Solomon, David's son who became king in the stead of his two (dead) older brothers, wrote these words: "Beware my son of the harlot, for her bed is the gates of Sheol (Hell) and those who go in do not return" (Proverbs 7:21–27).

Where did this statement come from? Did David share the pain of his decision with his son? Did he tell Solomon that he destroyed his family and sold the lives of his children for a few moments of pleasure? Do these words reflect the focus of a lesson about faithfulness to God's purpose in making him king over being distracted by the power and privilege of the throne? I believe that these are David's words and that Solomon wants each of us to know that, ultimately, we have only two choices. Either A David will lead from the front, or he will get caught from behind.

Life Lesson: Lead from the front, or get caught from behind.

David always led his men to victory from the front of the battle; that is, until the day that he sinned with Bathsheba. It was when he decided to take it easy and hang back, that he got caught from behind, and he, his family, and his ministry never recovered. It is not that you can't rest. Seasons of rest are essential to your health and ministry. Just don't rest in the time when you should be at war.

So where did David go wrong? Scripture does not give us that answer, but it seems that somewhere David began believing that the anointing made him special instead of responsible. It is obvious from his actions that he felt above God's Law, so he did as he desired instead of what God willed.

So how do you avoid this kind of destruction? The answer is surprisingly simple. The things that will keep you safe and separated from sin and the destruction it will bring are the things that got you here in the first place. It's about remaining a true worshipper of the God you love. That's it. Worship produces a God-centered lifestyle that will keep you faithful when your lesser passions try to overcome your true passion.

Principle 9: A David must allow his worship to produce a life lived in true submission to God and the principles of His kingdom found in His Word, the Bible.

A David is a worshipper. This worship permeates his life and considers every decision with a look toward his Shepherd for direction. God, as his Shepherd, will guide as He needs, not always as David desires. A David must then choose to follow God and not lesser passions. This ensures that he will see the full realization of the destiny for which God created him, instead of holding only the crumbling shell of broken dreams that remains after compromise.

Where are the Davids?

CHAPTER 10

Absalom

Purpose, Potential, but No Product

Absalom was David's son. Though the third oldest chronologically, Absalom seemed to have David's charisma and anointing to lead people. The picture that scripture draws is one of an incredibly handsome young man with long flowing hair and a regal air, who seemed to inspire an admiration and loyalty from people that had not been seen since David's early years. More than that, Absalom seemed to have been David's favorite son. He was the heir apparent to the throne, yet it was never to be.

David's sin with Bathsheba was not just a sexual sin. He had Uriah, her husband, placed on the front lines and ordered that he be left to die at the hands of the Ammorites. David had murdered him to cover his sin, and then he took Uriah's wife as his own. These acts of sin were not just against Uriah and Bathsheba but against God and His commandments. The effects were catastrophic. David had sown violence and murder, and now he would reap the harvest of his actions. "The sword will never leave your house" was the word David received from Nathan the prophet, and sadly his words came true.

Life Lesson: You will reap what you sow, regardless of your position or anointing.

Your anointing does not change spiritual laws. Sowing and Reaping is a spiritual law, so make sure that your lifestyle sows good seed. A harvest is coming, and you will reap what you have sown. David's sin with Bathsheba was sexual. Driven by his unrestrained lust, David imposed his desires on a woman who could never be lawfully his. What he sowed, he also reaped.

Amnon, David's eldest son, also imposed his desire on a woman who could never be lawfully his when he raped his half-sister Tamar. To most of us this level of perversion seems unimaginable. Can you imagine David's rage at this act of violation against his little girl? So what did David do to address his son's sin? Did he expel him from the kingdom, sending him to Israel's equivalent of Siberia? How did David punish Amnon? You're going to be shocked at the answer. He did *nothing*. Even with Tamar devastated and shamed beyond words by what her brother had done to her, her father, the king, did nothing.

When something like this happens, the victim just wants to be cared for and protected by those she loves most, but that's not what Tamar got. Honestly, I wonder if that's why she never got over it. When she needed the healing that comes from the loving care of her father, she got nothing. The results are equally tragic because Tamar, the beautiful daughter of the king, never married. She never had children. After her brother's betrayal and her father's ineptitude, she was left with nothing—nothing except one strong shoulder to cry on, the shoulder of her big brother, Absalom.

Two years later, Amnon was dead, murdered at a feast by his half-brother Absalom who ran for his life and found refuge in the house of his grandfather, the king of Geshur. He remained there for three years until David invited him back home, but again his father did nothing and refused to see him for two more years. During this time of isolation from his father, Absalom's bitterness toward David grew until he had devised a plan. He'd overthrow and disgrace his father. He would be a good king and unlike David, he would establish a throne of justice for the nation of Israel, where victims would find restitution and the criminals would be punished. Whereas his father had not acted justly with Bathsheba or for his sister Tamar, Absalom would be a king who would establish God's Law and rule in righteousness. He would be a good king, unlike his father.

The kind of grace that was on Absalom can barely be understood by us today. A parallel might be seen in the intense admiration that the American people had for John F. Kennedy Jr. Young, handsome, charming—all the best of his father, with the grace of his mother. This was the way the people saw Absalom. It appears that he would have been the next king if only he had waited. Rebellion is never the path to the throne because it cuts out the wilderness and the purification it brings to the heart and its motives. This is important because entering the throne—even the throne to which we are called—before we are ready only leads to destruction. Rebellion is never the answer for A David. That is true, *even* when the authority that God has set over you is in the wrong.

So what happened here? How could Absalom, this amazing son of David destined for greatness, become a rebel against his own father? The answer is simply, bitterness.

Bitterness is the worm that will eat the apple of your soul from the inside out. Bitterness is the rot of the belly that hungers only for vengeance. Nobody wants to be bitter but bitterness will come. Its seed is the injustice of the sin committed against you. One day, everyone will be violated by another, and the sin of bitterness will knock on the door of the soul and ask to come in. Like David that day on his rooftop, you have a choice. Bitterness is inviting. It feels good to allow it to come in and sit by your side as together you devise the plans to avenge the wrongs done to you. It feels good to imagine the destruction of the one who has brought so much destruction to your life and to the lives of those you love. It feels good, but like an addict shooting up, it feels good for a while but in the end it will only destroy you. The difference between David and Absalom is simply this: David chose worship. Absalom chose bitterness.

Life Lesson: Every David can become, instead, an Absalom.

What makes the difference between the two is what you do with your hurt. A David chooses to look up, raising his eyes from his circumstances and worship his God. That's why he is able to forgive the Sauls who hunted him. An Absalom chooses to live with his hurt until bitterness becomes like an old friend, until it's all that he sees. How do you stop this? Forgive. Forgivness is a choice to give a person something they don't deserve. You choose to set them free from their debt to you, but the offender is not the only one you set free. You see, when you forgive another you'll find that you become free yourself. Forgive, and let God give you life again; otherwise, you will die an embittered soul. David or Absalom—the choice is yours.

Both David and Absalom had the opportunity to be angry and hurt. Saul pursued David in the wilderness like a rabbit chased by wolves. David had failed his family, first in sinning with Bathsheba and then in not dealing directly with Amnon's sin against Tamar. The difference is that David chose to honor God and the king that God had established in Israel. Twice David could have killed Saul. Twice he chose to let Saul live. David would not lay his hands on the man that God had anointed as Israel's king (1 Samuel 24; 26). David's worship refused to allow bitterness to live in his heart. Instead, he loved Saul, and wept when he heard of the death of the king in battle (2 Samuel 1:11–12). Absalom chose the opposite path. Instead of valuing God and his authority invested in a flawed human being, Absalom invited bitterness in and rebelled against his father. In this decision, this young David became instead an Absalom; he became David's opposite.

Life Lesson: The opposite of A David is an Absalom.

True opposites are subtle things. It's not usually a heads-or-tails difference. The opposite of a David is not the shepherd boy who became a shepherd man. In fact, a true opposite is very nearly exactly like what it opposes. The only difference is, a reflection in a mirror, they are exactly the same, except left is right, and right is left.

I believe that Absalom was called to be the first David, but he failed in his wilderness of pain. He missed his Kairos Moment. Instead of being faithful, he became vengeful. Instead of his heart being purified through his trial, it became putrified. Instead of cultivating a heart of worship to push back the darkness, he allowed the darkness to enter his heart so that it was all he could see. Hurt was not what caused Absalom's rebellion. Instead, it was Absalom's response to that hurt that caused the rebellion. Every David can become an Absalom. The difference is only in whether you will choose to forgive or choose to become bitter. Your destiny is wrapped up in the decision that you make.

The end of this story is no better than its beginning. Absalom's rebellion was put down after an extended period of civil war, and he was killed. Ironically, he literally was caught by his pride when his long, flowing hair caught in the limbs of a low hanging tree, suspending him there between heaven and earth until a spear found his heart. It wasn't supposed to end like that. None of this was supposed to end like that, but that is the fruit of sin. Sin is a choice, and when we choose to sow destruction, a harvest of destruction will follow. The Law of Sowing and Reaping never fails. Be careful what you sow.

There might be no person in the Bible more tragic than Absalom. Samson? Maybe. Judas Iscariot? You could argue that, but I would say that no other person is as tragic as Absalom. He was Daddy's boy, the favorite son of the legendary king. His gifts and charms were unparalleled by anyone in the kingdom and maybe in the entire Bible. He was going to be the next David, but instead he chose bitterness over blessing. Instead of allowing this wilderness to catapult him into Reign, it took his life. This is your choice too. Will you allow your wilderness to ruin you, or will you become A David?

Principle 10: A David chooses, through the pain, to submit to God's rule and process in his life.

Jesus said, "In this world you will have trouble but be encouraged. I have overcome the world" (John 16:33). A David sees the process of purification in the pain, and so he chooses to allow God to bring him through "the valley of the shadow of death," instead of choosing to live there. A David, like the other Bible hero Joseph, does not take matters into his own hands, even when he has the power to do so. Instead, he relies on God to work through the evil to bring about good (Genesis 50:20). A David chooses to worship God, even in the wilderness.

Where are the Davids?

CHAPTER 11

The Mighty Men

The Legacy of a David

David was a leader of epic proportions. He inspired not only those who were part of his Kingdom but people throughout the ages. The reason is that David was a giant-killer.

David the Giant-Killer

From the moment David burst onto the scene in ancient Israel, he was the ideal picture of the victorious underdog. It was that victory over Goliath that propelled David into the national spotlight and made him the subject of the folklore for ages to come. It was also that victory, along with many others, that made David a man whom others wanted to follow.

If You Want to be a Giant Killer, Hang Out with One!

An elite group of warriors are recorded in 2 Samuel 23:8–39. They are classically referred to as David's Mighty Men, but in the scriptures they are called the "Thirty Chiefs" or simply "The Thirty." These were King David's Special Forces, and facing any of these thirty-seven men (there weren't exactly thirty) was a death sentence to the enemies of the throne. Here are some of their highlights:

Josheb was the chief of the chiefs, and for good reason. He once killed eight hundred men with a spear in one battle. Eleazar and Shammah were next in line, each winning huge battles against massive odds. These are "The Three" and represent David's closest and most trusted warriors and friends. What most people don't realize is that it wasn't just their abilities on the battlefield. These were the men who came to David while he was hiding from Saul in the Cave of Adullam. Abishai became a commander with "The Three," because of his incredible abilities as a warrior. He once killed three hundred men with his spear in a battle, but, and this is important, he *never* became one of them.

Life Lesson: Old friends are the best friends.

When a friend has been with you through the best of times and the worst of times, you know he will never leave you. There may be others who have great abilities, but the one who has been faithful to you through it all is the person you can trust, knowing that even when the rest of the world is against you, he will stand by your side.

Benaiah was a "bad man," with the kind of warrior highlights of which legends are made. He once killed two mighty warrior brothers in the same battle. Another time he climbed into a pit and killed a lion on a snowy day. In case you were wondering, you generally don't want to face a lion, but if you do, you *definitely* don't want to face one on a snowy day in a pit. Finally, he killed an "impressive Egyptian." More impressive than that, he killed the dude *with his own spear.*

These five men, as great as they were, are only a sampling of the warrior greatness in David's Mighty Men, yet there is an important story missing—the story of a giant-killer. In the Bible, several giants were defeated. The armies of Israel defeated the kings of Sidon and Og; both were giants. Caleb, Moses's only faithful spy beside Joshua, along with his family faced and killed giants in taking his mountain home in the Promised Land. Though as a nation Israel has a history of killing giants, very few warriors killed giants on their own. Two of the warriors on that list are David and Elhanan.

Elhanan is mentioned only a few times in the Bible. In 1 Chronicles 20:5 and 2 Samuel 21:19, he is described as the man who killed Goliath's brother, who had a spear the size of a weaver's beam (let's just say it was huge). Elhanan is mentioned only one other time in the scriptures when he is listed as one of David's Mighty Men (2 Samuel 23:24).

Eagles Don't Hang with Chickens

There was something in David that drew out the best in others. The exploits of David's Mighty Men weren't the same, but the victorious spirit, which drove them, was. It was the spirit of their leader, the spirit of a man who risked it all for the people of Israel and the God they served. It was the spirit of David, and it became part of them.

Leaders Lead

I have a saying—"Leaders lead"—but this saying has gotten me in trouble since the first time I said it. That little gem left my mouth during a conversation with a prominent ministry leader who was unwilling to take a risk. I listened as he described the difficulty in risking so much politically about a "touchy issue" that would ultimately determine the trajectory of an entire ministry organization. It was then that I said, "Leaders lead." Translation: "You're acting like a coward. If you don't want to lead, then get out of the way and let someone else stand up for God and His people and do what's right." The problem with saying that was that I was a young leader on his ministry staff ... oops.

David was a leader because he led. If someone is not leading, he *is not a leader*! It's as simple as that. If a leader is going to become A David, he must do more than just lead in a direction. He must become a leader of leaders, and that means he must be determined to grow those who follow him. A David does this in several ways.

- A David leads by example.

Leaders who are big on giving orders and short on executing their responsibilities are not leaders; they're only managers. Leaders lead by example. That means they lead from the front. If there's a job to do, they aren't too important to get their hands dirty along with their men. Instead they are right there in the middle of the fight with them.

- A David leads by training.

It's interesting that the Three came to David while he was hiding in the cave of Adullam. That's profound because only losers came to David when he was in that place of loneliness and isolation. You can read about it in 1 Samuel 22:1–2. It says that David attracted the "desparate, in debt or discontent." Out of this ragtag bunch arose The Three. That means that if they were to become some of the greatest warriors in the history of Israel, David had trained them to become those legendary warriors. A David shares what he knows so that he can grow warriors for God's kingdom.

- A David leads by sharing his victories.

There are times when leading from the front will get you in trouble. In fact, if you haven't trained your warriors, it'll get you killed. Second Samuel 21 tells the story of a giant set on killing David, and he almost had him until Abishai came to his aid and killed the giant. If you fight all the battles on your own, you will eventually grow tired and die. Worse, you will never grow other warriors. A David gives the opportunity for young men to fight alongside him and to share in the victory so that they can eventually win their own.

- A David leads by sharing his sorrows.

In David's times of great sorrow, it seems that it was his men that gave him comfort and direction. Sometimes that came from a kick in the butt, while other times it came by allowing David to see what he needed to do next. Don't be afraid to let those young leaders closest to you see your wounds and scars because it removes you from the pedestal and reveals that you are just like them—human.

- A David leads by sharing his life.

The Three, the most elite of The Thirty, became David's dearest and most trusted warriors and friends because they had shared his life. They were with him from the earliest days of his flight from Saul and remained with him to his last days on earth. Between those poles, David always knew this simple fact: These were "his boys." You only can have that with someone who is truly committed to you. Find people who love who you are first, and then invite them into the deeper places of your life. Will some hurt you? Yes, but if you end up with three lifelong friends that you can truly share your life with, it's worth the disappointments.

Lead. Train. Share your victories. Share your life, and raise up leaders with your spirit. Raise up giant-killers! That is the legacy of a David.

Principle 11: A David leads his Mighty Men to raise up the next generation of giant-killers.

A David leads. His leadership blazes a trail that others willingly follow to become the next generation of leaders in the kingdom of God. This kind of leadership is costly. You must give yourself to your people, bringing them close to you so that they may see your life and know what it means to be A David. The end result is the impartation of your spirit into their lives. The end result is a new generation of Davids.

Where are the Davids?

CHAPTER 12

Solomon

The Redemption of Your Greatest Mistake

And we know that in all things God works for the
good of those who love him, who have been called
according to his purpose.

—Romans 8:28

In this book we have looked at the life of David as a model
showing each of us how we too can come into all that God has
called us to be. The difficulty is that, to a point, we have seen
only an idealized picture of King David. Don't misunderstand
me; all the things I've written are a prophetic interpretation of the
story of the biblical David, but even the scriptures give us only
a basic view of one of the greatest and yet most complex men in
history. David was truly a great man, but he was also just a man.
I believe that this is one of the reasons David is so loved by so

many. He is so human. In fact, no one else in the Bible is such a raw reflection of what it means to be human. In so many ways, David is the embodiment of our greatest values. I mean, who is more courageous than David? When he faced Goliath that day, everyone thought he was completely insane for fighting a fully armed giant with nothing but a sling and five stones, but then ... he won! Even today, his victory inspires each of us to attempt the impossible.

Yet this same man committed adultery with Bathsheba and had her husband killed to cover up his sin. The man who was "after God's own heart" failed—and failed epically. David was messy, and because of that, he became the encapsulation of our greatest ideals and our darkest natures. Above all else, he was an amazing and deeply flawed *human*.

If we look at ourselves honestly, all of us will realize that we have lived lives that have been less than what God really wanted for us. The problem with books like this is that it sounds like X + Y = Z. The problem is, if we do X + Y, we don't always get Z because life is much more of an "A to Z," and we make a lot of decisions between those two points. We may regret some of those decisions, so what do we do with that? What if we have a Bathsheba, and it produces an Absalom? Is it over? Does God just quit on us? These are the questions that can keep us up at night.

With that said, this final chapter is an encouragement to everyone who hasn't lived the perfect life (yeah, the line starts behind me). I want you to hear this very clearly: God is not limited by your greatest mistake. In fact, the Bible says that He makes all things work together for our good (Romans 8:28).

God knows this life is hard. Remember that Jesus lived a fully human life. Some people have wondered why Jesus had to pray if He was God in flesh. The answer is simpler than most realize. Jesus had to pray to God while in this human form because no man can survive this world without prayer to the Father. In fact, the scripture says that He was tempted in every way, yet He remained sinless (Hebrews 4:15). Jesus was tempted because He was a man. In other words, He knows how it feels, so He is compassionate on us.

Jesus is on our side. Though we know that's true, there is usually still that little voice that accuses us, whispering, "Yeah, but what about those mistakes you chose to make?" It's then that our minds become like a computer infected with a virus, popping up all of the memories of all the things we wish we'd never done. As we see those things, we feel guilt, shame, and even self-hatred. Our minds scream, "What about those things?"

Well, God wants us to know that He will make even our worst mistakes become a blessing—*if* we just keep walking and following Him.

> Even though I walk through the valley of the shadow of death,
>
> I will fear no evil, for you are with me ... (Psalm 23:4)

In some ways, David's story may seem like it ended after his sin with Bathsheba. It's true that his meteoric rise leveled off after this sin, but David's life was far from over. He ruled Israel with effectiveness and blessing for many years after Absalom's rebellion, until his death as an old man. Bathsheba even became David's wife! They had kids of their own, and one of them was named Solomon.

Solomon became the next king of Israel after David died, and *that's* the message. David's sin cost him more than any of us could ever know. Uriah, Bathsheba's husband, was dead, along with two of David's sons. Tamar never recovered. The carnage seems to never end, but then we remember Solomon. Solomon's rule was the greatest period in Israel's history. It is said that during his reign, Israel was so wealthy that silver was like pebbles in the streets (2 Chronicles 1:15). Solomon brought peace to all of Israel's borders. His wisdom is legendary, but that's not all he's known for.

Solomon built the temple in Jerusalem, giving God a permanent home in this world for the first time. Not only that, but God's promise that a son of David would reign on Israel's throne forever—a promise that will ultimately be fulfilled in Christ—was first fulfilled in Solomon. Solomon was incredible. He was a gift from God, so as you read about his exploits, remember this: *Solomon was the son of Bathsheba.* So in a very real way, had David not sinned with Bathsheba, Solomon would never have been born. The greatness that we see in Solomon was the direct result of David's greatest failure.

The point is simply this: No matter what you have done, God can take your greatest mistake and make it the thing that ultimately becomes your greatest gift to the world.

Principle 12: A David never quits.

Even in failure, A David never quits walking with God. He knows that the One he's following redeems, recovers, and reconciles all things, making all things work for his good—even his biggest mistakes.

Where are the Davids?

CONCLUSION

Zion

The Place of Reign

Zion

Zion might bring to mind stories about God and of King David, who cherished God's presence, but what is Zion? Biblically, more than any other thing, Zion is synonymous with God's presence. Zion is Zion because God is there.

The first time we hear the name Zion, it is a part of the city of Jerusalem, the capital of the Jebusite nation. Zion was Jerusalem's fortress and was considered impregnable. After David took Jerusalem, this fortress became the place where he lived. It was named the City of David, and it was here that he established his throne and ruled the nation of Israel. What's funny is that piece of information is often overshadowed by the fact that Zion was the place that housed the presence of God in the Tabernacle of David.

Tabernacle of David

David was a worshipper. He loved the Lord and spent his life telling Him so through the writing of psalms and a life lived to serving God and His people. More than anything, David wanted to be near God's real presence, and that presence hovered over the Ark of the Covenant.

> You make known to me the path of life; in your
> presence there is fullness of joy; at your right hand
> are pleasures forevermore. (Psalm 16:11 ESV)

When David became king, the Ark of the Covenant was in Shiloh. The Ark was a gold-covered box that had held the stone tablets that contained the Ten Commandments, Aaron's staff, and the Manna that had fed Israel in the wilderness. If you've ever seen *Raiders of the Lost Ark*, the Ark of the Covenant is what they were looking for. Unlike in the movie, though, the Ark was not some magical talisman. It was the place where God's presence shimmered in a cloud over the cover of this box, called the Mercy Seat. This "seat" was, in very real way, God's throne on earth.

Many times the Ark led God's people into military victories or into new territories to receive His promises to them. When the nation of Israel crossed the Jordan River to march on Jericho, it was the Ark, on the shoulders of the priests, that first entered the river and created dry ground for the entire nation to cross into their Promised Land. During the time of conquest, Joshua, Moses's successor, had set Shiloh as the center of government and administration. The Tabernacle of Moses, home of the Ark, found a permanent dwelling there so Shiloh became Israel's worship center (Joshua 18:1). It was here that David had to travel to be near the physical presence of God. It was only twenty miles from Jerusalem, but in ancient Israel, it was an entire day's journey. Being so far from God's presence was not okay with the king, so he made a command:

> Let us bring the ark of our God back to us, for
> we did not inquire of it during the reign of Saul."
> The whole assembly agreed to do this, because it
> seemed right to all the people. So David assembled
> all Israel, from the Shihor River in Egypt to Lebo
> Hamath, to bring the ark of God from Kiriath
> Jearim. (1 Chronicles 13:3–5)

David brought the Ark to Zion and created a place of worship called the Tabernacle of David. This tabernacle was different from the Tabernacle of Moses in one crucial way. Instead of worship being centered around blood sacrifice and atonement for sin, the Tabernacle of David was a place of praise and worship to God. This is an important difference. You see, the Tabernacle of Moses paid for Israel's sins so that God could live among His people (Exodus 25:8; Levitcus 16:32–34). The focus was on how bad humans were and how perfect God was.

David's tabernacle was different. Instead of worship being centered in rituals that cleansed people from sin, the Tabernacle of David was a place of praise and worship that focused on celebrating the greatness of our God and the privileged relationship we have with Him as His people. It was more than just a new place for God to dwell. It was a place for Him to be exalted!

This kind of worship became the access point for God's people into a new dimension of worship, and it changed the game forever. We even see this in the New Testament. As God began to save people from among the idol-worshipping nations outside of Israel, James, the half-brother of our Lord Jesus, said,

> "Brothers, listen to me. Simeon has related how God first visited the Gentiles, to take from them a people for his name. And with this the words of the prophets agree, just as it is written, "'After this I will return, and I will rebuild the tent (tabernacle) of David that has fallen; I will rebuild its ruins, and I will restore it, that the remnant of mankind may seek the Lord, and all the Gentiles who are called by my name, says the Lord, who makes these things known from of old.' (Acts 15:13–18 ESV)

If you are a Christian and are *not* Jewish, you are part of the rebuilding of this tent… the Tabernacle of David! How awesome is that?

With that in mind, here are some things you need to know about the Tabernacle of David in Zion:

- It was not the highest place in Israel because God wanted worship to be accessible to anyone.

- It was the place where the people of Israel came three times a year to worship the Lord as a nation.
- David designed special instruments and choirs to give praise to God 24/7/365 days a year, in this tabernacle.
- The Tabernacle of David was the home of the Ark.
- It also appears to be the place where David's throne was found.

For our purposes the last point may be the most important. If David reigned from the Tabernacle of David, then the place of David's worship was also the place of David's reign.

Life Lesson: The place of your worship is also the place of your reign. Why? Because you reign through your worship.

This is the point of this concluding thought. In fact, this is the point of this book. You can only reign for God through your worship.

Every Christian is called a king and priest (Revelation 1:6; 5:9–10). Kings have thrones and reign from them. Priests worship and act to bring God and people together. Since this is true, you need to know that your reign is tied to your worship.

God created you to be A David, a king that He would establish to reign for Him in this world, to extend His kingdom, and to bring salvation to people. You are literally an extension of Jesus's ministry on earth today. Because you are called to be A David, you have to establish your reign through worship and relationship, just as David did. You have to rule from Zion. In this way you will become truly like David in that you will establish a throne for Jesus to reign on through your life. The fact is that our King, the Lord Jesus Himself, will reign from Zion, seated upon David's throne. Ultimately, that is why He was born.

> And the angel said to her, "Do not be afraid, Mary, for you have found favor with God. And behold, you will conceive in your womb and bear a son, and you shall call his name Jesus. He will be great and will be called the Son of the Most High. And the Lord God will give to him the throne of his father David, and he will reign over the house of Jacob forever, and of his kingdom there will be no end." (Luke 1:30–33)

Today we are called to do the works of Christ and even greater works than He did while living here on earth (John 14:12). That starts with creating a place of worship where God can establish His kingdom and reign in this world. Your life of worship creates that throne, allowing Jesus to reign through you. That is why you are called to reign. Whether in business, government, education, entertainment, sports, or world missions, God created you to be A David. The only question that remains is whether or not you will accept the call. Will you? Will you become A David?

Concluding Principle: A David is a king who reigns through worship.

A David is a child of God and because of that, he is a king and a priest in this world (Revelation 1:6; 5:9–10). Kings have thrones from which they rule a region, and priests worship. For A David, his throne and reign is founded upon his lifestyle of worship.

Where are the Davids?

CPSIA information can be obtained
at www.ICGtesting.com
Printed in the USA
LVHW111322160720
660862LV00001B/297